1 MONTH OF
FREE
READING

at

www.ForgottenBooks.com

By purchasing this book you are eligible for one month membership to ForgottenBooks.com, giving you unlimited access to our entire collection of over 1,000,000 titles via our web site and mobile apps.

To claim your free month visit:
www.forgottenbooks.com/free953688

ISBN 978-0-260-52168-2
PIBN 10953688

Historic, Archive Document

Do not assume content reflects current scientific knowle
policies, or practices.

1901

Nathan Smith & Son

WHOLESALE FLORISTS,

x   x   x   ADRIAN, MICH., U. S. A.

MRS. ELMER D. SMITH.

A Complete List of the Latest Novelties.

TO OUR PATRONS. ✗ ✗

 ❧ ❧ We take pleasure in handing you our Chrysanthemum list for 1901, and accept this opportunity to thank you for the very generous patronage conferred the past season. We shall use every effort to make each shipment satisfactory, by supplying only first-class stock, and treating each customer as liberally as such quality and and our moderate prices will allow. Each year we receive new customers through the recommendation of our patrons. We consider this the very best form of advertising and thank all who have shown such interest in our behalf. If you have friends who are interested in the class of plants we offer, please send us their addresses, and it will be duly appreciated.

☞ READ CAREFULLY BEFORE ORDERING, THE FOLLOWING TERMS OF SALE.

All previous quotations are canceled by this list.

Not less than **five (5) plants of one variety** at 100 rates, and where dozen rates are given to novelties and scarce varieties, **six (6) at dozen** and **twenty-five (25) at 100 rates.**

We do not **bind ourselves** to these prices **after June 1st,** as there is often a decline or advance, according to supply and demand. In case stock of certain varieties is exhausted, we reserve the **right to decline** the order.

While we **exercise** the **greatest care** in executing all orders to keep our stock **true to name,** we give **no warranty, expressed** or **implied,** and **cannot guarantee** or be in any way **responsible for the crop,** either as to **variety** or **product.** Should errors occur, do not fail to **report at once,** as we **cannot** entertain claims of **long standing.**

All orders are filled in **strict rotation,** carefully labeled, lightly and securely packed, and delivered to the carriers **in good condition** free of charge.

Cash, or satisfactory reference must accompany **all orders** from unknown correspondents. You can **save money** by sending **cash,** as we allow **five (5) per cent. discount** where remittance accompanies the order. If discount is not deducted, we will include extra plants to cover the amount. All accounts are **due and subject to draft in sixty (60) days,** unless otherwise agreed upon.

Those desiring goods shipped **C. O. D.,** are requested to advance a sufficient amount to assure us they will be accepted on delivery. We **ship** all plants by **Express** unless otherwise instructed, but where impracticable, we will forward by Mail post-paid all orders of fifty cents and upward.

Our shipping facilities are excellent, having direct connections with **all parts of the country. We guarantee** our shipments to be delivered at the **special plant rate,** which is 20 per cent. less than the rate on merchandise.

When ordering, please mention a few additional varieties. These will be sent **only** in cases where the stock of those ordered is exhausted.

To **avoid errors** and **delays,** make your order on a **separate sheet,** using only **one side,** and **one variety** on a **line.** To this add your **Name, Post-Office** and **State plainly written,** also give **Street Number** or **P. O. Box,** if any.

☞ In all cases the foregoing terms will be strictly adhered to.

Soliciting the continuance of your valued patronage, we remain,

Yours very respectfully,

NATHAN SMITH & SON.

New Chrysanthemums for 1901.

Descriptions of Nathan Smith & Son's Novelties.

Our persistent efforts to improve the Chrysanthemum have been crowned with success. Each year bestows new awards for the new candidates. We believe our success is due to the care we take in selection of parentage, with the view of securing marked improvements. When you consider that we are the originators of such kinds as Iora, Niveus, Nyanza, Modesto, Mrs. M. A. Ryerson, Mrs. J. J. Glessner, Sunstone, Merula, Western King, Midge, Merza, Rustique, Idavan, Xeno, Nagoya, Monrovia, Orizaba, Intensity, White Bonnaffon, Lavender Queen, Goldmine and Superba, all of which are classed among the best, not only in this country, but abroad, it is evident that we are in touch with the needs of all Chrysanthemum growers.

We consider **Iolantha** the best early pink yet produced. **Omega** is an extra large, second early yellow. **Mrs. Elmer D. Smith** is an improvement on Maj. Bonnaffon. Although the last mentioned variety failed to secure the Chrysanthemum Society

IOLANTHA.

Cup by one point, yet it outscored all competitors, receiving the highest number of points before that Society's Committees. This fact is worthy of consideration when ordering novelties. We commend the following:

Price, 50c each; $5.00 per doz.; $35.00 per 100. Ready April 1st, 1901. Not less than 6 at dozen and 25 at 100 rates. Orders filled in strict rotation.

Iolantha.—An incurving pink maturing Oct. 10th to 15th. Fine stem and foliage; height 3½ ft.; good from either bud, although second crown (about Sept. 5th) comes a few days earlier. Color a beautiful shade of soft pink. We consider this the best early pink yet produced. Certificated by C. S. A.

Omega.—A second early yellow, ~~the same shade~~ as Mrs. J. J. Glessner; 7¼ in. in diameter. Belongs to the V. Morel type, but has broader petals. In perfection Oct. 25th. Certificated by C. S. A.

Mrs. Elmer D. Smith.—Of the many fine seedlings we have produced ln-the last ten years, this one possesses more points of excellence than any of its predecessors. A Jap. Inc. of the most perfect form; full, double, high rounded center. Bright yellow, deeper than Golden Wedding. In the C. S. A. Cup Contest at Chicago, it stood second, falling only one point behind the winner. The blooms in this exhibit were 7 in. in diameter. Stem and foliage perfect; scant 3 ft. high. This variety will rival Maj. Bonnaffon, being brighter in color, more dwarf, very similar in form, with much heavier and stronger stem. In season Nov. 1st to 10th. Four of the C. S. A. Committees gave this variety an average of 92.75 points.

Pompons.

Price, 25¢ each; $2.50 per doz. Ready April 1st, 1901.

Nita.—A beautiful rose pink; extra fine, full double flower of the large flowering class. Height 2 ft.

Vera.—High rounded flower; Dahlia-like petals. White, slightly tinted blush; large flowering. Height 2¼ ft.

Acto.—Very perfect flowers of the large flowering type. Incurving Dahlia-like petals. Bright rose with lighter reverse; 2¼ ft. high.

Yezo.—A small flowering variety of very perfect form; 1 in. in diameter; ball shape. Blush; 2 ft.

Zenta.—Very bright crimson maroon; full double flowers of perfect form; small flowering; 2¼ ft.

Nydia.—Pure white, high rounded flower; extra fine form; large flowering. In perfection Oct. 25th; 3¼ ft.

Garda.—Small flowering; dwarf; 1¼ ft. high. Pure white; very desirable for small pot plants.

Novia.—Delicate pink; Daybreak Carnation color. Very perfect form. In perfection Oct. 25th. Height 3¼ ft.

OMEGA.

Mizpah Seedlings.

The merits of Mizpah as a dwarf decorative variety are well established and these new colors of this distinct type will be valuable additions. They are all of the same dwarf habit, not attaining more than 12 in. in height, with small single Marguerite-like flowers.

Argenta.—Pure white.

Zeroff.—Yellow.

Rosina.—Light pink.

Double Mizpah.

Phallena.—Same general character as Mizpah, producing small, double flowers; color magenta pink, same as the parent.

Novelties from Various Sources.

Six at dozen; twenty-five at 100 rates. Ready April 1st.

Brutus.—(May.) Very bright red, shaded with orange. Broad, reflexed petals. A large, handsome flower; extra good stem and foliage; 3 ft. Crown or terminal bud; mid-season.' C. S. A. Cert. 50c ea.; $5.00 per doz.; $35.00 per 100.

Chestnut Hill.—(May.) Clear, bright yellow, of excellent form and substance. Flat petals, reflexed and incurved. A seedling from W. H. Lincoln; 3 ft.; terminal bud. Season, Nov. 25th to Dec. 10th. C. S. A. Cert. 50c ea.; $5.00 per doz.; $35.00 per 100.

Gen. Antonia Maceo.—(Robt. Laurie.) Result of a cross between Cullingfordii and Geo. W. Childs. The flowers are about the size of Shrimpton and of the same color, but unlike that variety, does not sunburn or fade. It is exceedingly dwarf and must be propagated very early to attain the height of 3 ft. The best crimson in existence for single stem pot plants. It has much larger and heavier foliage than Shrimpton. Last crown or terminal. 25c ea.; $2.50 per doz.

Golden Beauty.—(Hill & Co.) A reflexed sport from the popular variety H. W. Rieman, having the same dwarf habit and rich yellow color. Owing to its reflexed form, it produces a much larger flower than Rieman. 35c ea.; $25.00 per 100.

Lady Roberts.—(Pierson & Co.) From the same cross as Timothy Eaton, which it very much resembles, in fact several experts, who have seen both in growth and bloom, consider Lady Roberts superior. Stem and foliage are all that can be desired. Second crown or terminal. 50c ea.; $5.00 per doz.; $30.00 per 100.

Malcolm Lamond.—(Hill & Co.) A very dwarf red, same color as Fisher's Torch, but an improvement in every way. Perfect foliage; 2½ ft. high. The easiest of its color to grow. Does not burn. C. S. A. Cert. 35c ea.; $25.00 per 100.

Mary Hill.—(Hill & Co.) Raised by H. W. Rieman. A seedling from Mme. F. Perrin, of similar habit and growth, but very much fuller, showing no sign of a center. A light shade of pink, with a high pearl gloss on outer petals. In season Nov. 15th. C. S. A. Cert. 35c ea.; $25.00 per 100.

Mrs. W. B. Chamberlain.—(May.) Outer petals drooping, center incurving. Color, a lovely shade of pink. Distinct, both in color and form. Good stem and foliage; terminal bud; midseason. C. S. A. Cert. 50c ea.; $5.00 per doz.; $35.00 per 100.

Timothy Eaton.—(Miller & Son.) The sensational novelty of the year. An enormous, globular Jap. Inc. variety of perfect form and growth. Color, pure white. A seedling from M. Wanamaker. In season Nov. 15th; 4 ft. high. It captured every cup and prize for which it was entered, also C. S. A. Cert. 50c ea.; $5.00 per doz.; $30.00 per 100.

Yanariva.—(May.) V. Morel form. Blush pink; very striking; seven inch blooms. Terminal bud; midseason. A grand acquisition. C. S. A. Cert. 50c ea.; $5.00 per doz.; $35.00 per 100.

Zampa.—(May.) Old gold; reverse, bright strawberry red. Lower petals tubular, balance flat. Fine for exhibition. Terminal bud; 3 ft. 50 ea.; $5.00 per doz.; $35.00 per 100.

Novelties of 1900.

Price, 10c each; $6.00 per 100, except where noted. Not less than 5 plants of a kind at 100 rate.

Bonita.—A beautiful deep golden orange, shaded with light bronze. A large, rounded flower. Excellent stem and foliage. Midseason. 10c ea.; $5.00 per 100.

Col. D. Appleton.—A very large, deep golden yellow Jap. Inc. flower, of fine finish and form. Excellent stem, with foliage up to the flower, and an easy grower. Terminal bud only. This variety was in nearly all the prize-winning collections last Fall, and is destined to become one of the best commercial varieties introduced for years. 10c ea.; $8.00 per 100.

Eulalie.—Anemone flowered. Pure white; broad petals. A valuable addition to this class. 10c ea.; $5.00 per 100.

Florence E. Denzer.—A very late Jap. of good habits. In season Dec. 20th and after. Color, lilac pink, with waxy white reflex; dwarf. Best described as a very late Pink Ivory in color, growth and form, but the flowers are not as deep. 10c ea.; $5.00 per 100.

Goldmine.—Unsurpassed in size, having been grown 11 in. in diameter. Resembles Sunderbruch in foliage and general habit. 3 ft. high. Rich golden yellow; outer petals reflexed and center incurving in a whirl. Best from second crown. At its best Nov. 20th. It brought the highest market price on Thanksgiving day. It was also a prize-winner in many of the late shows. 10c ea.; $8.00 per 100.

H. J. Jones.—One of the largest crimsons to date, the average diameter being 8 in. Reflexed on the style of V. Morel and just as double. 4 ft. high; rather early. 10c ea.; $8.00 per 100.

Hon. W. F. D. Smith.—Brilliant glowing crimson; very large, with good stem and foliage; 3¼ ft.

Intensity.—Reflexed form, showing only the bright crimson upper surface of petals. Slender stem, but sufficiently wiry to carry the flower erect; 4½ ft. high. Winner of many prizes, both as a cut flower and bush plant.

GOLDMINE.

Height 3 ft. This variety was the best early, large yellow on the market last Fall.

Lavender Queen.
A large Jap.; outer petals reflexed and center petals erect, making a flower of great depth. Good stem and heavy foliage; height 3 ft. In color a pleasing shade of lavender pink, decidedly distinct. The largest and finest pink for Thanksgiving trade, being at its best on that date. This variety has given entire satisfaction and is highly recommended by all who grew it.

Lady Anglesey.—A sport from Chas. Davis. The color is a true shade of dark bronze, with no trace of yellow. 10c ea.; $8.00 per 100.

Luciole.—Broad, incurved petals; color, a beautiful combination of pink cerise and lavender. Good habits; 4 ft.; midseason. 10 ea.; $5.00 per 100.

Marguerite—Creamy white, Jap.; similar to Frank Thompson, but earlier. Luxurious foliage and stiff stem. Oct. 25th; 4 ft.; either bud. 10c ea.; $5.00 per 100.

Monrovia.—A large, bright yellow early Jap. variety, with heavy stem and foliage. Form of Bergman but much larger. Flowers same date as M. Henderson, but is an improvement in every way.

Nesota.—A Jap. variety of the largest size. Long, broad strap petals loosely arranged, giving a very artistic appearance. Dwarf, sturdy, short-jointed growth, with heavy foliage. Color, light yellow. Midseason. A very fine exhibition variety, owing to its large size.

Orizaba.—A beautiful midseason Jap. Inc. of a pleasing shade of light pink. Its dwarf, sturdy habit, perfect stem and foliage and ease of culture will give it first place, either as a commercial or exhibition variety. It won first prize at Chicago in competition with the best standard pink varieties. 10c ea.; $8.00 per 100.

Pluma.—One of the most perfect of this type; color, very delicate pink. Very double, closely incurved blooms. 10c ea.; $8.00 per 100.

Primo.—A very large, clear white Jap. variety of perfect habit, flowering first week in October. It promises to become a very popular early white.

Souci.—Very large blooms, and extra good stem and foliage. Jap. Inc.: bright, clear yellow; midseason; 4 ft. 10c ea.; $5.00 per 100.

Superba.—The best Christmas flowering variety to date. A very double, high built flower 6 in. in diameter. It may be termed a perfectly double Maud Dean (one of its parents), having the same upright growth and fine foliage. Color, bright pink. Height 4 ft. Take only terminal bud. The most profitable late Chrysanthemum now in commerce.

Walter Molatsch.—Very fine second early yellow Jap. Inc., which may be briefly described as an early Wm. H. Lincoln. Very dwarf, sturdy habit and fine foliage. Large blooms of good substance. Extra fine for early exhibitions, owing to its large size.

LAVENDER QUEEN.

White Bonnaffon.—Color, pure white; form identical with Bonnaffon; growth and general habits same as Robinson (one of its parents.) In season Nov. 20th and after. Take terminal bud only. This is another valuable Thanksgiving variety. Its lateness, combined with above good points, give it a prominent place among commercial varieties.

Winona.—Base of petals white, with veins of deep pink running through the outer ends. A full flower, and an excellent keeper. Good stem and foliage. 10c ea.; $5.00 per 100.

Yellow Fitzwigram.—A yellow sport from Lady Fitzwigram. The earliest yellow on the market. 10c ea.; $4.00 per 100.

European Novelties.

Ready April 1st.

Last year's importations included many meritorious varieties, both from exhibition and commercial point of view. The following foreign collection is the best we have ever offered. Several have been awarded certificates and others were in prize-winning collections. If you desire to be a successful exhibitor next Fall, do not fail to include these. Note our special prices in collections.

Annie Prevost.—Pure white; similar to Ivory in growth and height. Flower, same shape as Nagoya.

J. R. Upton.—A bright yellow Australian variety, in form similar to Mme. Carnot. Large and double; dwarf, sturdy growth.

Mdlle. D'Estienne.—A very large, pure white flower, style of Niveus. Strong growth and heavy foliage. Comes highly recommended as an exhibition variety.

Mme. Deis.—A monster white variety. Extra fine, both for commercial and exhibition blooms. Has good stem and fine foliage. Second crown bud.

Mme. VonAndre.—(Yellow Mutual Friend.) A light yellow sport from Mutual Friend, identical except in color.

Miss Alice Byron.—A pure white variety, with very broad, loosely incurving petals, similar to Mrs. H. Weeks. Dwarf and robust.

Mrs. Ritson.—A beautiful white sport from V. Morel. C. S. A. Cert. 50c each; $5.00 per doz.

Mrs. Coombes.—An enormous reflexed flower, with very broad petals; in color a beautiful shade of bright rose. Very dwarf, short jointed growth, with large, luxuriant foliage. A splendid acquisition, either for commercial or exhibition blooms.

MRS. RITSON.

Mrs. Barkley.—Very large flower. with possibly the broadest florets of any Chrysanthemum yet raised. Long florets, soft rose, silvery reverse. Dwarf, sturdy habit and very easy grower.

Nellie Pockett.—A grand new variety, originating in Australia. An extra early white Chrysanthemum of mammoth size, larger than Col. D. Appleton and earlier than Mrs. H. Robinson. Creamy white Jap., with long, drooping florets, curling at the tips, making a very solid, compact bloom on the style of Mayflower, but very much superior. A fine, healthy grower. with grand stem and foliage. Equally valuable for commercial and exhibition purposes.

Princess Bassaraba.—An extra fine, pure white flower of enormous size. Very stiff stem; foliage well up to the flower; medium height. C. S. A. Cert. 35c ea.; $25.00 per 100.

T. Carrington.—A Jap. Inc. of enormous size, measuring 7 in. in diameter and about the same in depth. Color, magenta rose with silvery reverse. Use second crown bud. Grand for exhibition.

Walleroo.—An Australian seedling of decided merit. Very large, slightly incurving blooms, style of Niveus. Very broad petals; color, rosy cerise. A fine exhibition variety.

Price, 35c. ea.; $3.50 per doz., except where noted. One each of the thirteen varieties for $3.50.

Etoile de Feu.—Yellowish bronze; style of V. Morel. Dwarf, sturdy grower. Fine for exhibition.

Lord Cromer.—Very long, broad drooping florets, incurving at the tips. Rich, rosy crimson; 4 ft. Good for exhibition.

Miss Maud Douglas.—Large Jap. Inc.; dark rose pink, lighter reverse. Style of flower and growth similar to Xeno.

Madeline Davis.—A lovely and most distinct Jap. variety. White ground, overlaid and striped magenta; very unique. Morel form. Good substance.

Miss Annie Hills.—Inc.; color, blush pink; good growth.

Miss May Manser.—New early flowering, creamy white Jap., style of Marie Louise. Short, sturdy growth.

M. Louis Remy.—Light yellow sport from Mrs. C. H. Payne.

M. de Marcere.—Hairy; very large and double. Lower petals quilled and open at tips, center incurving; yellowish bronze. Louis Boehmer growth.

Mme. Noël Martin.—Creamy white Jap., center slightly incurved; large flower. Easy grower.

Salome.—Jap. Inc.; carmine, tinted rose; fine dwarf habit.

Sunset.—Golden orange Jap.; recommended for Christmas flowering; dwarf.

Souv. de Pierre Desblanc.—Jap. Inc., loosely arranged; rosy carmine.   Good habits.

Price, 25c each; $2.50 per doz. One each of the twelve varieties for $2.25. One each of the twenty-five in European collection, $5.25.

TWO ODDITIES OF SPECIAL MERIT.
25c each; $2.50 per doz. Ready April 1st, 1901.

Curly Locks.—Outer petals tubular and reflexed. open at the tips. luner petals incurving irregularly, forming a bloom of decided artistic effect. Color, a beautiful pink, changing to waxen white in the center. Can be grown 12 in. in diameter. Of very easy culture. No collection complete without it.

CURLY LOCKS.   PETALUMA.

Petaluma.—A grand flower, both in color and form. The petals are quilled and about the size of a large knitting needle. Very double flowers, and when fully developed are as round as a ball and 9 in. in diameter. Color, a very even shade of light bronze. A grand variety.

·General Collection.

Early.
5c each; $3.00 per 100, except where noted.

Adele.—A delicate pink Jap. Inc. Fine stem and foliage. A good early commercial pink.

Geo. S. Conover.—A fine early yellow variety. Large flowers; splendid habit and stem.

Geo. S. Kalb.—Pure white; style of Bergman, but larger; very double. Excellent stem and foliage; dwarf habit. Can be had very early.

Glory of Pacific.—The very best early pink to date. Dwarf, sturdy growth.

Harry A. Parr.—A lemon yellow Jap., with good stem and foliage.

H. L. Sunderbruch.—A grand early yellow, both for cut flowers and plants. Growth and general habits are perfect. 10c ea.; $4.00 per 100.

Independence.—An ever-blooming Chrysanthemum. Double flower, style of Bergman. Opens creamy, changing to pure white. Dwarf habit.

Ivory.—A pure white flower of globular form. The most popular early white.

J. E. Lager.—Very large, reflexed light yellow. Exceedingly strong growth. Good.

John K. Shaw.—A Jap. Inc. commercial pink with excellent stem and foliage. One of the best in its color.

Kate B. Washburn.—A white sport from Mrs. E. G. Hill. Very useful.

Kuno.—A broad petaled, white Jap. variety, much larger than Bergman and flowers at the same date. Dwarf, robust habit. The earliest large flowering white.

Lady Fitzwigram.—The first good early white on the market. Dwarf habit.

Lady Playfair.—A good second early pink. Large globular flowers of good substance.

Marquise de Montemort.—The earliest good pink to date, flowering same time as Lady Fitzwigram. Moderately tall, but good stem.

Marion Henderson.—An early, large reflexed yellow. Fine for cut flowers.

Merula.—Very double Jap. Inc. Beautiful shade of light pink. Dwarf; semi-early. 10c ea.; $4.00 per 100.

Merry Monarch.—A creamy white, large, spreading flower. Still very popular.

Midge.—The best dwarf early white. Excellent stem and foliage. Resembles Bergman, but is an improvement, being much larger. 10c ea.; $4.00 per 100.

Mme. F. Bergman.—A very popular early white. A favorite with many.

Mrs. J. Lewis.—Very large, pure white flowers of reflexed form. This variety is becoming very popular with many growers. 10c ea.; $4.00 per 100.

Mrs. Seulberger.—Pure white, general style of Ivory. Very perfect in form and of large size. Compact, sturdy growth.

Mrs. E. G. Hill.—A very large, early pink variety of the Jap. Inc. type. Good stem and foliage, and of easy culture. Second crown or terminal bud. One of the best.

Mrs. F. L. Button.—Very large, pure white flowers of the Jap. Inc. type, flowering early in October. Good grower.

Pink Ivory.—(Agnes L. Dalskov.) A beautiful pink sport from Ivory.

Polly Rose.—A pure white sport from Glory of Pacific. The same ideal growth.

Pride.—A large, early commercial white, coming in with M. Henderson. Reflexed bloom, borne on a stiff stem and having a short neck.

Robt. Halliday.—This is one of the finest second early yellows introduced for several years. A large, broad petaled Jap. flower, with perfect stem and foliage. Dwarf habit.

Soleil d'Octobre.—(October Sunshine.) A yellow Jap. of good substance and excellent habits, coming in flower a few days later than Robt. Halliday. Very short-jointed growth with heavy foliage. An ideal commercial variety. 10c ea.; $4.00 per 100.

Willowbrook.—An early white Jap. variety of good substance; good stem and foliage. An improvement on Merry Monarch. 10c ea.; $4.00 per 100.

Yellow Monarch.—A canary yellow sport from Merry Monarch.

Yellow Queen.—A Jap. Inc. flower of good substance and large size. Yellow from crown bud, lower petals bronzy from terminal. A great favorite.

Midseason.

5c each; $3.00 per 100, except where noted.

Admiral Dewey.—A large Jap. Ref. Deep chrome yellow, similar to Thornden.

A. H. Fewkes.—Bright yellow Jap.; dwarf grower. Excellent for bush plants.

Australian Gold.—Light yellow Jap. Inc. of large size. Good grower. Feed sparingly.

Autumn Glory.—Very large Jap. flower on the style of V. Morel. Deep salmon, changing to soft shrimp pink. A fine exhibition flower.

Black Beauty.—Very dark red; dwarf, sturdy grower. 10c ea.; $4.00 per 100.

Black Hawk.—Dark crimson scarlet; style of V. Morel. Long, strap petals regularly arranged. Best from terminal bud. An extra fine commercial red.

Boule d'Or.—A very large incurving flower; color, golden buff. Dwarf habit.

Bruant.—An immense reddish-bronze Jap. Inc. Stem and foliage, large and very heavy. A first class exhibition variety.

Buff Globe.—Buff, shaded orange. A sport from Good Gracious.

Capt. Gridley.—White, sometimes shaded delicate blush. A high built Jap. Inc. flower of the largest size. Late midseason.

Chipeta.—A Jap. Inc. of extraordinary size. Color, quite similar to that of ripened oak leaves. Exhibition.

Chito.—Strap petal; fine red stripes on yellow ground, giving a bronzy appearance. Good stem and foliage. This variety should be in every exhibition collection.

Chas. Davis.—A light bronze sport from V. Morel, possessing same excellent habit.

Chempwec.—A clear, bright yellow sport from Silver Cloud.

Col. W. B. Smith.—A grand exhibition variety when properly grown. Broad, incurving petals; golden bronze.

Dorothy Spaulding.—Large, massive Jap. Inc. blooms, in perfection Nov. 20th. Deep rose pink, shade of Maud Dean. Dwarf, sturdy grower. 10c ea.; $4.00 per 100.

Elmer D. Smith.—Cardinal red, reverse chamois; broad petals. Very large.

Eugene Dailledouze.—A very popular yellow. Large globular blooms.

F. A. Spaulding.—A yellow sport from Mayflower. An improvement on Yellow Mayflower, being much darker in color. 10c ea.; $5.00 per 100.

Fee du Champsaur.—Pure white Jap. flower with long, broad petals. Good stem and foliage. An excellent exhibition variety, being in many of the prize-winning collections.

Fisher's Torch.—Pure deep red; flat petals, of a satiny finish. Does not burn easily.

Francois Coppie.—A large Jap. flower. Chrome yellow, striped with red; good habits. Best from second bud. Exhibition. 10c ea.; $5.00 per 100.

Frank Hardy.—A pure white sport from Good Gracious. Take crown bud only.

G. J. Warren.—(Syn. Yellow Mme. Carnot.) A yellow sport from Mme. Carnot. Very fine for exhibition.

Geo. W. Childs.—An exquisite shade of bright crimson. Give high cultivation until buds are formed and do not feed thereafter. 10c ea.; $4.00 per 100.

Golden Wonder.—Old gold, with deeper shading at center; broad, reflexed petals. Dwarf, robust growth. An exhibition variety of large size.

Gold Standard.—Form, color and style of Golden Wedding; one of the largest.

Golden Gate.—A very large golden bronze, with broad strap petals. One of the best for exhibitions.

Golden Shower.—Without doubt one of the most distinct and unique Chrysanthemums. The florets are as fine as hair, 4 in. to 5 in. long, drooping and interlacing like corn silk. Color, yellow, intermingled with red and bronze petals. Dwarf habit and of easy culture. No collection is complete without it. 15c ea.; $10.00 per 100.

Golden Wedding.—Enormous reflexed flowers; color, bright yellow. One of the most popular commercial and exhibition varieties. 10c ea.; $4.00 per 100.

Good Gracious.—A well known exhibition variety of large size. Soft pink. Quilled petals, irregularly incurved.

Helen Bloodgood.—A very beautiful shade of true, clear pink. Rather tall.

Henry Weeks.—A rosy crimson Jap. of immense size; broad petals. Dwarf habit; perfect stem and foliage. This variety was very prominent in many of the exhibitions. 10 ea.; $5.00 per 100.

Hicks Arnold.—Although an old variety, it is still extensively used for pot plants. Golden bronze; moderately early.

H. W. Longfellow.—A broad petaled, incurving white variety of fine form. Stiff stem and beautiful foliage. Rather early.

Idavan.—A very large, compact Jap. Inc. flower of the Mrs. H. Robinson type. Lower petals delicate pink and the center creamy white. Perfect stem and foliage. Unexcelled as an exhibition variety.

Iora.—An exceedingly artistic flower of light pink color. Petals tubular their entire length, incurving in a whirl. Fine for exhibition. 10c ea.; $4.00 per 100.

Jeannie Falconer.—(Syn. Peter Kay.) A very large lemon yellow exhibition flower. Dwarf; good stem and foliage. A prize-winner at many shows.

J. H. Troy.—A very good second early white. Perfect form and habit.

John Shrimpton.—Very dwarf; excellent for pot plants; same color as Geo. W. Childs. 10c ea.; $4.00 per 100.

Lady Byron.—Broad, incurving, ivory white petals. Dwarf habit. Early.

Lady Hanham.—A sport from V. Morel. Cerise pink, shading to gold. Beautiful pink under artificial light.

LeGrand Dragon.—Very large orange yellow flower, with long, drooping petals on the style of Mme. Carnot. Good grower; 5 ft. 10c ea.; $5.00 per 100.

Marie Calvat.—Jap. Ref.; in color a delicate shade of pink. Splendid dwarf habit and an abundance of foliage. A valuable exhibition variety. 10c ea.; $6.00 per 100.

M. B. Verlot.—Very large Jap. Inc. with long, broad petals. Color rose mauve. Good habits. One of the largest of this type and a valuable addition to the exhibition class. 10c ea.; $6.00 per 100.

Maj. Bonnaffon.—Very soft, clear yellow, of perfect Inc. form and dwarf habit. The most popular Chrysanthemum to date.

2

Mayflower.—An irregular flower of large size; creamy white. Fine for exhibition.
Marg. Jeffords.—One of the best exhibition bronzes. A large incurved bloom.
Merza.—An extra large pure white Jap. Inc. bloom. Owing to its dwarf habit and perfect foliage, it is unexcelled for pot culture. 10c ea.; $6.00 per 100. Ready April 1st.
Meta.—White, delicately shaded lemon at base of petals. Jap. Inc.; robust, compact grower.
Mizpah.—It has no equal for decorative work. Single; color, bright rose; height 12 in. to 16 in. Its very dwarf habit and freedom of bloom makes it exceedingly desirable for show houses.
Minnie Wanamaker.—A pure white Jap. Inc. Can be had late. An old standby.
Minerva.—Large yellow Jap. Inc. Quite extensively grown as a pot plant.
Miss Georgienne Bramhall.—A very pleasing shade of straw yellow. Beautiful incurved form. Moderately early.
Miss Georgiana Pitcher.—A bright yellow Jap. Inc. variety of perfect form. Heavy, short jointed growth with foliage close to the flower. Crown bud.
Miss Florence Pullman.—A loosely arranged white Jap. flower of large size.
Mme. E. Roger.—The nearest approach to a green Chrysanthemum now in cultivation. A broad petaled Jap. flower, outer petals creamy white, center light green. Good stem and foliage. Very attractive. 10c ea.; $5.00 per 100.
Mme. Carnot.—Very large pure white Jap. A prize-winner. 10c ea. $4.00 per 100.
Mme. F. Perrin.—An extra fine globular flower of a pleasing shade of bright pink.
Modesto.—Rich yellow Jap. Inc. flower of large size. The best of its color.
Monstrosum.—Jap. of globular form, with tubular petals; magenta pink. Second bud.
Mrs. A. J. Drexel.—Bright crimson lake; best of its color. 10c ea.; $4.00 per 100.
Mrs. Geo. West.—Immense Jap. Inc. Rosy purple. 10c ea.; $4.00 per 100.
Mrs. F. A. Constable.—A pure white sport from Iora. This variety attracted much attention and won prizes at many of the shows. 10c ea.; $4.00 per 100.
Mrs. J. J. Glessner.—Light yellow, with apricot shadings. A large flower of excellent keeping qualities, making it especially desirable as a show variety and for bush plants.
Mrs. M. A. Ryerson.—A pure white Jap. of distinct form. Narrow petals, reflexed from crown bud and irregularly incurved from terminal. Extra fine.
Mrs. H. Weeks.—Beautiful white Jap. Inc.; very broad petals. A valuable variety, being especially suitable for bush or single stem pot plants.
Mrs. S. C. Probin.—Clear pink Jap. Inc., with silvery reverse. Excellent dwarf habit. Suitable for any purpose. 10c ea.; $4.00 per 100.
Mrs. Trenor L. Park.—A valuable addition to the exhibition class. Clear, bright golden yellow Jap. Inc., center incurved and lower petals reflexed, forming a globular flower of the largest size. Short jointed growth. 10c ea.; $4.00 per 100.
Mrs. W. Mease.—A sulphur yellow sport from Mme. Carnot, which is thoroughly distinct from the yellow sport J. G. Warren.
Mrs. J. Peabody.—Very large Jap. of fine form and finish; pure white.
Mrs. C. Lippincott.—Very bright yellow exhibition variety. 10c ea.; $6.00 per 100.
Mrs. Geo. A. Magee.—A large Jap. Inc. flower of perfect form; pinkish lilac.
Mrs. W. H. Rand.—A peculiar flower with thread-like petals; bright yellow.
Mrs. W. C. Egan.—A very large Jap. Inc. exhibition flower of special merit. Color, creamy white, suffused with pink. Excellent stem and foliage. Rather early.
Mrs. H. Robinson.—A large, pure white Jap. Inc. variety. Good for all purposes. Too well known to need further description.
Mrs. O. P. Bassett.—A light yellow sport from Mrs. H. Robinson.
Mutual Friend.—A large spreading flower of the purest white; dwarf. Extra.
Niveus.—Grand white of easy culture; valuable for all purposes. Can be flowered late.
Nyanza.—Broad, incurving petals so arranged as to show both the crimson scarlet lining and golden reverse. 10c ea.; $4.00 per 100.
Pennsylvania.—A sport from Philadelphia; Bonnaffon color. 10c ea.; $4.00 per 100.
Peter Kay.—(See syn. J. Falconer.)
Phenomenal.—A very large exhibition variety of the Jap. Inc. type. Color, buff, with darker shadings. Perfect stem and foliage.
Philadelphia.—Incurved petals; creamy white, shading to primrose at tips. No collection complete without it. 10c ea.; $4.00 per 100.
Pitcher & Manda.—Tubular petals; inner portion of flower yellow, while the outer rows of petals are white. Very unique. 10c ea.; $4.00 per 100.
Pride of Ryecroft.—A light yellow sport from the popular variety Niveus.
Red Warrior.—A valuable addition to the exhibition class, either for cut flowers or bush plants. Jap. Color, chestnut red. Perfect growth; rather early.
R. Hooper Pearson.—Large, broad petaled flowers, slightly incurved and in color a very deep golden yellow; early midseason. Stem, foliage and general habits are perfect. Undoubtedly the best foreign variety of recent introduction. 10c ea.; $6.00 per 100.
Rough Rider.—Very large Jap. Inc. pink. An excellent exhibition flower. 10c ea.; $4.00 per 100.

Rustique.—A bold, incurved flower of the largest size. Color, a distinct shade of golden brown. Extra fine for all exhibition purposes. 10c ea.; $4.00 per 100.

Shavings.—A curiosity. Medium sized flowers, which are like a mass of curled mahogany shavings; dwarf and early.

Shilowa.—A brilliant crimson Jap. of easy culture and good habits. The petals are twisted and contorted, but show only the dark crimson upper surface, making a very artistic and showy bloom. Liquid manure should be withheld after the buds are formed.

Silver Cloud.—Delicate salmon pink. A Jap. exhibition flower of fine form.

Silver Wedding.—A large, pure white reflexed flower of good substance. Very broad petals, some being nearly one inch in width. Rather tall. Terminal bud.

Simplicity.—A pure white reflexed exhibition variety, equal to Mme. Carnot in size.

Solar Queen.—Golden yellow with lighter shadings. Perfect growth. Extra.

Spottswood.—A beautiful high built incurved light yellow. Good grower.

Sunstone.—Style of The Queen. Bright yellow, shading to red at base, light straw reverse. Perfect habits. Pleasing and distinct. Valuable for exhibitions.

The Bard.—Large, full flowers, reflexed form. Bright red. Fine for bush plants.

The Queen.—A very popular exhibition white. Jap. Inc.

The World.—One of the largest Chrysanthemums ever produced. Long, straight petals, slightly incurving toward the center. 10c ea.; $5.00 per 100.

WHITE BONNAFFON.

Thornden.—A bright yellow Jap. of large size. Feed sparingly. Very good.

T. H. Spaulding.—Broad petaled Jap. Inc.; deep red. Extra fine growth.

V. Morel.—Bright pink Jap. Grown by all. 10c ea.; $4.00 per 100.

Western King.—Pure white Jap. Inc. flower, outer petals slightly reflexing. One of the finest whites. Can be had very late from late cuttings. 10c ea.; $4.00 per 100.

Yellow Mayflower.—A lemon yellow sport from Mayflower.

Yellow Mme. Carnot.—(See syn. G. J. Warren.)

Late.

5c each; $3.00 per 100, except where noted.

C. H. McCormick.—An immense flat flower. Color, bronze.

Clara Goodman.—Color and style of H. W. Rieman, but more reflexed. Good.

Eclipse '98.—A light yellow sport from Wm. H. Chadwick. 10c ea.; $4.00 per 100.

Ed. Hatch.—Very large globular flowers, outer petals recurving slightly. Color, creamy white with pink shadings.

E. M. Bigelow.—A very good late red. Broad, incurving petals.

Harry Balsley.—Unequaled among pinks. Rather tall. Terminal bud.

Henry Nanz.—A sport from Mrs. J. Jones. Light yellow, shaded bronze. 10c ea.; $4.00 per 100.

Heron's Plume.—Pure white. Opens flat, incurving into irregular, varied forms at maturity. Very distinct.

H. W. Rieman.—Its dwarf habit and fine high rounded flower of bright yellow color, gives this variety a prominent place in this class.

Invincible.—A large, incurving white, sometimes tinted pink. Very desirable. 10c ea.; $4.00 per 100.

Liberty.—Best very late yellow to date. Buds taken Oct. 10th and after will give good flowers for Christmas. Dwarf, sturdy grower. 10c ea.; $6.00 per 100.

Maud Dean.—With many the most popular late pink. 10c ea.; $4.00 per 100.

Mdlle. Lucie Faure.—A closely incurved flower of perfect finish. Color, pure white. Fine for late exhibitions. Good habits.

Merry Christmas.—A large flat flower, which is at its best Dec. 20th and after. One of the best late whites. 10c ea.; $4.00 per 100.

Mrs. Geo. F. Baer.—(See syn. Yellow Mrs. J. Jones.)

Mrs. S. T. Murdock.—Good for all purposes, especially large specimens. Excellent stem and foliage. Color, soft pink.

Mrs. Jerome Jones.—The most popular late white with many. It may be had as late as Christmas when planted late. An excellent shipper.

Nagoya.—The best yellow for Thanksgiving. Very large Jap. Ref. blooms, same color as Modesto. Heavy stem and large, dark foliage up to the flower. Being of easy culture, it is especially valuable as a late variety.

Pres. W. R. Smith.—A pleasing shade of light pink; vigorous habit; tall.

Quito.—An even shade of light pink; style of Maud Dean, but more double. An extra good late pink. Best from terminal bud.

Rinaldo.—Crimson, with old gold reverse. One of the best of its color.

Tuxedo.—Bright orange amber. Useful as a bush plant. Very distinct.

V. H. Hallock.—A beautiful Jap. variety of good substance; color light rose. A very fine late pink.

W. H. Lincoln.—Bright yellow. A well known variety and one of the best.

Wm. H. Chadwick.—A very large Jap. Color, white, occasionally striped pink. In perfection Nov. 25th and after. This variety should be grown by everyone. 10c ea.; $4.00 per 100.

Xeno.—The best late Jap. Inc. pink yet disseminated. It has the color of Perrin, the same dwarf habit, good stem and foliage, but is larger and perfectly double. A closely incurved flower on the style of Ivory. At its best Thanksgiving time and after. An ideal commercial flower. Take terminal bud only.

Yanoma.—A very late pure white; petals long and loosely arranged. One of the best.

Yellow Mrs. J. Jones.—A sport from Mrs. J. Jones. Color, similar to Bonnaffon. 10c ea.; $4.00 per 100.

Anemone Section.

10c each; $4.00 per 100.

Ada Strickland.—Symmetrical; light chestnut red; full and high center; ray petals broad, flat and regular.

Condor.—Very large; tubular rays; rosy purple, tipped yellow.

Delicatum.—Long, delicate blush guard petals, pure cream disc; high center.

Descartes.—Bright crimson red. Dwarf habit. Extra fine.

Enterprise.—Ray florets, light rose; sulphur yellow center. Fine form.

Eulalie.—(For description and price see Novelties of 1900.)

Falcon.—White rays, shaded pink; pale straw yellow center. Medium size.

Garza.—Single row of broad ray petals; well formed center. White, tipped yellow.

Halcyon.—An extra large, pure white Anemone. Broad guards, with high center.

Jas. Weston.—White ray petals; center, lemon yellow. Small flowered.

John Bunyan.—Lemon yellow; long, fluted guard petals; darker center. Very full.

Junon.—Blush pink. Cushion, extra large and dense.

Marcia Jones.—Immense snow white flowers of perfect form. Solid rows of guard florets with high cushion center.

Mrs. F. Gordon Dexter.—Double row of white rays; center, deep rose pink. One of the largest in this class.

Queen Elizabeth.—Silvery blush; long ray florets; center, tipped yellow.

ZORAIDA.

San Joaquin.—Light lemon yellow center, pure white guards. One of the best.

Satisfactio.—Deep chrome yellow, suffused with gold and amber. Wide open trumpet-like florets; guard petals, broad and flat.

Surprise.—Very large flowers; forked and hooked guard petals; high center; pink florets; distinct. The best of its color.

Thorpe, Jr.—Pure golden yellow. Extensively used as an exhibition flower.

W. W. Astor.—Long, flat guard petals; white, sometimes tinted blush; high golden center. Especially fine for bush plants.

Zoraida.—A huge Jap. Ane. The ray florets are white; some entirely tubular, others half tubular, finishing with a strap tip. Pure yellow center. A very artistic and striking flower.

Incurved Section.

10c each; $4.00 per 100, except where noted.

Adula.—A late white, with good stem and foliage. An easy grower of medium height. This is a valuable addition to the late commercial varieties. 5c ea.; $3.00 per 100.

Arline.—Pure white; dwarf habit; excellent stem and foliage. Bonnaffon form. One of the best of its class. 5c ea.; $3.00 per 100.

Belle Poitevine.—Small, pure white flowers of perfect form. Unequalled for sprays or informal bush form. 5c ea.; $3.00 per 100.

Chas. H. Curtis.—Large, deep, perfectly incurving flowers; rich golden yellow.

C. W. Ward.—Extra large snow white flowers, solid and perfect in form.

Lorelei.—Very solid; medium size. Center white, lower petals lilac pink. Good growth.

Lord Wolesley.—Bronzy red; perfect form; early and tall.

Mable Ward.—A very pleasing shade of yellow. Perfect formed flower.

Miss Gladys Spaulding.—Snow white; perfect form and habit.

Miss Lottie D. Berry.—Large, fine white; very double. Strong stem, with ample foliage.

Miss Louise D. Black.—Rich orange yellow; style of Maderia, but larger.

Mongolian Prince.—Large golden bronze; dwarf; makes a fine bush plant.

Mrs. R. C. Kingston.—Pearly white, suffused with pink. One of the best.

Oeta.—Bright yellow, shading to orange. Perfect in form; dwarf habit.

Rena Dula.—In perfection Oct. 10th. Dwarf; stiff stem. Color, deep pink.

Yonitza.—White, with delicate green shadings; perfect form. Very late.

Hairy Section.

10c each; $4.00 per 100, except where noted.

Beauty of Truro.—A purplish bronze sport from L. Boehmer.

Golden Hair.—Bright chrome yellow, suffused with amber. Very broad and closely incurving petals, densely covered with spines.

PLUMA.

Imp. Louis Boehmer.—A light pink sport from L. Boehmer.

L'Enfant des deux Mondes.—Grand white sport from L. Boehmer.

Leocadie Gentils—A bright yellow sport from "L'Enfant des deux Mondes." We consider this the best yellow hairy variety yet introduced.

Louis Boehmer.—Magenta pink. Good vigorous habit. Fine for bush plants.

Mrs. C. B. Freeman.—Sport from L. Boehmer: color varies from yellow to bronzy yellow, according to temperature.

Mrs. Higanbotham.—A large incurved flower with extremely wide petals. Bright pink.

Mrs. Marguerite Carbone.—White, shading to pink. Very compact in form.

Pluma.—(For price and description see Novelties of 1900.)

Queen of Plumes.—A beautiful shade of bright pink. In fullness, form and growth, similar to White Swan, only more dwarf. One of the best. 10c ea.; $6.00 per 100.

R. M. Grey.—(Syn. Hairy Wonder.) Terra cotta. The most distinct and best of its class. 10c ea.; $6.00 per 100.

White Swan.—This surpasses all the whites in this section. Closely incurved, high built flower, very heavily plumed.

Yellow Louis Boehmer.—(See Leocadie Gentils.)

New Pompons of 1900.

10c each; $5.00 per 100.

Agatha.—White, with blush pink center. An exceedingly attractive flower.

Almeida.—Pink, changing to white with age. A well built flower.

Angelique.—Pure white, high built flower; very compact and neat.

Atlas.—Bronze, shaded lemon; very large and deep; distinct.

Attila.—Deep orange maroon; very compact form; medium size.

Canova.—Deep orange bronze. A very showy flower.

Elberta.—Deep, but clear yellow; very distinct. Symmetrical flowers.

Ethel.—Blush white; medium to large; a great keeper.

Magnificus.—Very beautiful, pure white flowers, of large size and extra good form. Fine branching sprays. Good in every way.

Norma.—Very large P. Ane. Ray petals, deep bronze; clear yellow center.

Viola.—Deep violet. A very showy and distinct flower.

Zenobia.—Bright clear yellow of brilliant shade. A handsome flower.

Pompon.

5c each; $3.00 per 100.

Ada.—Deep, clear yellow. Small, but a very interesting and pretty flower.
Agnes C.—Light bronze. Good size and very showy.
Amelia.—Blush pink, beautifully tipped with clear yellow.
Black Douglas.—Rich dark crimson; perfect form. The best of its color.
Caritas.—Blush, shaded deeper pink in center and at the base of petals.
Delicatissima.—Lower petals Daybreak Carnation color, center deep wine.
Edna.—White. with pink shadings and yellow center; good size; well formed.
Golden Fleece.—Clear yellow: small flower; early and free. Very strong grower.
Golden Mdlle. Martha.—Bright golden yellow; large and fine; dwarf.
Jeanevieve.—Blush pink; large flower. Extra fine variety.
Julia.—Color. deep crushed strawberry red; fringed edges.
Mdlle. Martha.—Fine white; rather large; dwarf.
Mrs. Bateman.—Orange brown; large; very good.
Oneita.—Bright, clear yellow; well formed flowers of good size. Very showy.
President.—Dark violet rose. Good habits.
Santiago.—Deep bronze red; very distinct and of good size.
Souv. du Jersey.—Brilliant golden yellow. One of the best.
Wm. Kennedy.—Crimson amaranth; rather large.

Pompon Anemone Section.

5c each; $3.00 per 100.

Aglaia.—Blush. changing to white; large.
Antonious.—Golden yellow guard florets and disc; rather large; dwarf.
Astarte.—Amber; very perfect form.
Emily Rowbottom.—Blush white sport from Marie Stuart.
Firefly.—Bright scarlet with high center. A very distinct and striking color.
Manila.—Ray petals, deep cardinal red, with bright yellow quilled center.
Marie Stuart.—Beautiful light pink. Valuable for made-up work or vases.
Mildred.—Clear white. with blush edges to petals.
Mme. Chalonge.—Blush guard florets; blush, shaded with sulphur disc.
Mme. Montels.—White guard florets; yellow disc; dwarf.
Mme. Sentir.—White; beautiful high center.
Reine des Anemones.—Pure white. Very fine.
Rose Marguerite.—Deep rose. Very strong grower.

Early Hardy Pompon Section.

5c each; $3.00 per 100.

Bronze Bride,—Rosy bronze sport from Blushing Bride.
Duel de Perle.—Bright yellow. Very dwarf.
Frederick Marronet.—Orange, striped red.
Illustration.—White, shading to pink.
Mdlle. Elsie Dordan.—Soft lilac pink; very neat, full globular bloom; dwarf.
Mr. Selley.—Rosy lilac; dwarf, compact habit and very free.
Piercy's Seedling.—Orange bronze; dwarf, sturdy habit. A very useful variety.
St. Mary.—Pure white. Fine.

VARIETIES FOR SPECIAL USES.

For the benefit of our patrons who are unfamiliar with the merits of the different varieties, we append the following selections, which we consider best for the purpose mentioned:

BUSH PLANTS.—Rustique, Geo. W. Childs, Minerva, Georgiana Pitcher, W. H. Lincoln, Ivory, Pink Ivory, Red Warrior, The Bard, Louis Boehmer and its sports, Mutual Friend, Mrs. S. T. Murdock, Hicks Arnold, Maj. Bonnaffon, Mme. F. Perrin, John K. Shaw. Robt. Halliday, Soleil d'Octobre, V. Morel and its sports, Miss Florence Pullman, Mrs. H. Weeks, Intensity, Geo. S. Conover, Silver Cloud, J. Falconer (Peter Kay), Mongolian Prince and Arline.

SINGLE STEM POT PLANTS.—Rustique, Mrs. H. Robinson, Maj. Bonnaffon, Goldmine, Merza, V. Morel and its sports, Mme. F. Perrin, Col. D. Appleton, Mrs. T. L. Park, Ivory, Pink Ivory, Red Warrior, Geo. W. Childs, Merula, J. Falconer (Peter Kay), Orizaba, Boule d'Or, J. K. Shaw, Idavan, Soleil d'Octobre, Mrs. O. P. Bassett, Walter Molatsch, Mrs. Elmer D. Smith. (New.)

EXHIBITION BLOOMS.—Maj. Bonnaffon, Mrs. Elmer D. Smith, Walter Molatsch, Idavan, J. Falconer (Peter Kay), Good Gracious and its sports, Golden Wedding, Merza, Mrs. M. A. Ryerson, Mrs. J. J. Giessner, Col. D. Appleton, V. Morel and its sports, Rustique, Black Hawk, Chito, Georgiana Pitcher, Goldmine, Modesto, Mrs. J. Jones and its sports, Mme. F. Perrin, Pennsylvania, Philadelphia, Iora, Mrs. F. A. Constable, Orizaba, Lavender Queen, Western King, Bruant, Mrs. W. C. Egan. Intensity, Nesota, Shilowa, Phenomenal.

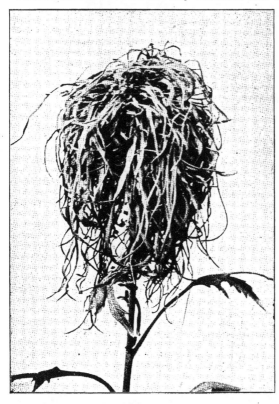

GOLDEN SHOWER.

CURIOUS VARIE-TIES.—Iora, Mrs. F. A. Constable, Mrs. W. H. Rand, Heron's Plume, Pitcher & Manda. Golden Shower, Shavings, Petaluma, Curly Locks, Mme. E. Rogers. The varieties named in the Anemone and Hairy Section, may also be classed as oddities.

Commercial Blooms.

(Based upon quality and ease of culture.)

EARLY.—White: Independence, Lady Fitzwigram. Pink: Marquise de Montemort. Yellow: Monrovia. Yellow Fitzwigram.

SECOND EARLY. White: Primo, Ivory, Polly Rose. Pink: Merula, Glory of Pacific, Pink Ivory, Iolantha (New). Yellow: Soleil d'Octobre (October Sunshine), Robt. Halliday, Walter Molatsch.

MIDSEASON.—White: Mrs. H. Robinson. Mrs. M. A. Ryerson, Niveus, M. Wannamaker. Pink: Orizaba, V. Morel, Mme. F. Perrin. Yellow: Maj. Bonnaffon, Yellow Mrs. J. Jones, Modesto, Col. D. Appleton. Crimson:, Geo. W. Childs, Shilowa.

LATE MIDSEASON.—(Nov. 15th to Thanksgiving.) White: Wm. H. Chadwick, White Bonnaffon, Western King. Mrs. J. Jones. Pink: Xeno, Lavender Queen, Mrs. S. T. Murdock. Yellow: Golden Wedding, Goldmine, Nagoya, W. H. Lincoln. Crimson: Intensity.

LATE.—(Thanksgiving to Christmas.) White: Merry Christmas, Yanoma, Invincible. Pink: Superba, Florence E. Denzer. Yellow: Liberty.

We have an immense stock of Chrysanthemums, and are therefore in position to quote special rates on large quantities for planting, during May, June and July, especially on the above list of varieties.
Should you desire varieties not listed, we will be pleased to hear from you, as our collection includes many not herein offered.

Carnation Novelties for 1901.

Ready for distribution February 15th, unless otherwise noted. Prices quoted are for STRONG, WELL ROOTED CUTTINGS. Not less than 6 at doz., 25 at 100 and 250 at 1,000 rate, except where noted.

Prosperity.—(Dailledouze Bros.) Formerly known and exhibited as No. 666. In habit, the nearest to the ideal yet produced, making no useless grass, but grows straight up to bloom. It attains a height of 4 ft. by Jan. 1st under no special culture. Very heavy foliage and stiff, upright growth. It is not subject to any of the Carnation diseases. The flowers attain the monstrous size of 4 in. Much freer bloomer than Mrs. Bradt and superior in all other points. It has the perfect calyx of Albertina. Entirely distinct in color, the ground being white, overlaid and mottled with pink, deepening toward the center. Its keeping qualities are unequaled. It has brought the highest price yet paid for a Carnation. Winner of numerous certificates and medals. 50c ea; $5.00 per doz.; $8.25 for 25; $10.00 for 50; $16.00 per 100; $130.00 per 1,000. Ready March 1st.

Gov. Roosevelt.—(Ward.) A seedling from the well known variety Gen. Maceo, which it somewhat resembles in habit, but a far more vigorous grower and longer and much stiffer stem. In color, a deep, rich, brilliant scarlet, heavily shaded with maroon. In form, it is as near perfect as any Carnation yet produced. Very large, full flowers, with perfect calyx, fully as good as that of Albertina. Very free, healthy grower. 25c ea.; $2.50 per doz.; $12.00 per 100; $100.00 per 1,000. Ready March 1st.

Norway.—(Weber & Sons.) A seedling from Mrs. Fisher. Color, purest white. Flowers 2¼ in. to 3¼ in. in diameter. A wonderfully vigorous, rapid grower of splendid habit. Responds readily to good culture. The stems are long, strong and graceful and can be cut 2 ft. to 3½ ft. long when well established. It is delightfully fragrant; an excellent keeper and shipper. We believe this variety will fill a long felt want. 15c ea.; $1.50 per doz.; $10.00 per 100; $75.00 per 1,000.

Egypt.—(Weber & Sons.) Color, a rich scarlet crimson. Outclasses all other crimsons we have grown. Its distinctive features are its grand color, which is just right for this shade, its exquisite spicy odor, its fine, commercial stem, which attains a length of 2½ to 3 ft., and the uniform large size of flower, averaging 2½ in. to 3 in. when established. Not recommended as being an early bloomer, but can be had in full flower Nov. 1st to 15th, after which it is a continuous and free bloomer. Recommended to all who are looking for a good dark Carnation. 15c ea.; $1.50 per doz.; $10.00 per 100; $75.00 per 1,000.

Lorna.—(Dorner & Sons Co.) Large, pure white, fragrant flowers, 3 in. and over in diameter. Well filled center, rounding the flower to a most pleasing form. Comparing it to White Cloud, its parent, it shows a decided improvement in its more compact and stronger growth; foliage of a much deeper, bluish tint, indicating hardiness; longer and decidedly stronger stems; larger flower, with perfect calyx; better form; purer white, and is an earlier and more continuous bloomer. It makes a strong field grown plant and transplants readily, even under unfavorable conditions. 20c ea.; $2.00 per doz.; $10.00 per 100; $75.00 per 1,000.

Mermaid.—(Dorner & Sons Co.) A fine formed bloom, of a pleasing shade of salmon pink.. Its easy cultivation, strong growth, fine, large flower, and being an early and extremely free bloomer, are its strong points. It has a medium strong stem early in the season, but improves rapidly during the Winter months. The weakness of stem when planted and a slight susceptibility to rust are its only faults, and prevent its being called a first-class variety. It can be successfully grown for Summer blooms in the field. 10c ea.; $1.00 per doz.; $6.00 per 100; $50.00 per 1,000.

Queen Louise.—(Dillon.) An extra fine white variety of distinctive qualities. A very strong, healthy grower and transplants easily from the field. Extra large flowers on long, stiff stems. In color, pure white with no shadings of any kind. Perfect, non-bursting calyx. Very fragrant. A good keeper and shipper. It is an early, free and continuous bloomer, which, added to its other good habits, makes it a commercial Carnation of exceptional worth. 15c ea.; $1.50 per doz.; $10.00 per 100; $75.00 per 1,000.

Dorothy.—(Mrs. Graves.) Bright, pure pink, about the shade of Scott, produces as freely as same and has no equal in keeping and traveling qualities. The flower is larger than Scott, finely formed and nicely serrated. This is not an exhibition variety, but as a money maker is unsurpassed. Good habits. 15c ea.; $1.50 per doz.; $10.00 per 100; $75.00 per 1,000.

3

General Collection.

6 at dozen; 25 at 100; 250 at 1,000 rate.

America.—Pure, soft scarlet of an even shade. Vigorous, compact grower, free from rust. Large flowers; strong calyx; stiff stem. Very free. First class in every way. 5c ea.; 50c per doz.; $3.00 per 100; $25.00 per 1,000.

Cerise Queen.—A very brilliant cerise. An improvement on Tidal Wave. Large flowers on strong, stiff stems. Very profuse bloomer. 5c ea.; 35c per doz.; $2.00 per 100; $15.00 per 1,000.

Chicago.—New of 1900. A bright scarlet sport from Mrs. Geo. M. Bradt. It is not very constant, but our stock has been carefully selected and is very near true. 10c ea.; 60c per doz.; $4.00 per 100; $30.00 per 1,000.

Daybreak.—Light salmon. The most popular Carnation of its color. 5c ea.; 25c per doz.; $1.50 per 100; $12.50 per 1,000.

Elsie Ferguson.—Burnt orange, occasionally marked with pink. The best of its color. Flower large; plant free in growth and bloom, of excellent habit. Good in every way. 15c ea.; 40c per doz.; $2.50 per 100.

Ethel Crocker.—New of 1900. This variety has taken first place among the best commercial pinks. Its freedom of bloom, extra large flower, long, stiff stem, strong growth and beautiful color, are making it a profitable Carnation everywhere. In color, a perfect shade of pink, brighter and deeper than Mrs. Jooste. Free from bacteria. 10c ea.; 60c per doz.; $4.00 per 100; $30.00 per 1,000.

Flora Hill.—A very large white, being a general favorite. A clean, healthy grower; long, stiff stems and a good keeper. The best white with many growers. 5c ea.; 25c per doz.; $1.50 per 100; $10.00 per 1,000.

General Gomez.—In color it surpasses all dark Carnations yet disseminated, being brilliant cardinal maroon. Large. full flowers on long. stiff stems, borne in great profusion. Resembles Scott in habit. 5c ea.; 35c per doz.; $2.00 per 100; $15.00 per 1,000.

General Maceo.—Very full, deeply fringed flowers on wiry stems. Color, brilliant scarlet, heavily overlaid with maroon. One of the darkest shades among Carnations. It is a very profuse and abundant bloomer. 5c ea.; 50c per doz.; $3.00 per 100; $25.00 per 1,000.

Genevieve Lord.—New of 1900. In color a beautiful shade of rose pink, a little darker than Albertina. It is of large size, perfect form and finish. Very fragrant. A free, continuous bloomer. The growth is vigorous and not effected by rust. We recommend this variety to all Florists. 10c ea.; $1.00 per doz.; $6.00 per 100; $50.00 per 1,000.

G. H. Crane.—The best scarlet Carnation to date, being very productive. A robust grower, having perfect calyx and strong stem, and producing very large flowers. 5c ea.; 50c per doz.; $3.00 per 100; $25.00 per 1,000.

Glacier.—A very pure white Carnation of dwarf habit and is an early, prolific bloomer. Excellent for design work, owing to its large size. 5c ea.; 35c per doz.; $2.00 per 100; $15.00 per 1,000.

Gold Nugget.—Large yellow, of good form and substance. The best of its color. 5c ea.; 50c per doz.; $3.00 per 100; $25.00 per 1,000.

Jubilee.—Very large, scarlet flowers; vigorous grower. The best scarlet Carnation with many. 5c ea.; 40c per doz.; $2.50 per 100; $20.00 per 1,000.

Mary Wood.—One of the largest whites. Good habits. The best white with many growers of fancy stock. 5c ea.; 40c per doz.; $2.50 per 100; $20.00 per 1,000.

Melba.—Large flowers. Color, beautiful rose pink, of a very even shade. Long, stiff stem and a very free, continuous bloomer. 5c ea.; 35c per doz.; $2.00 per 100; $15.00 per 1,000.

Morning Glory.—New of 1900. Color, slightly darker than Daybreak, but an improvement in every way. Large, perfect flowers on long, wiry stems. A very free, continuous bloomer, with no tendency to crop. This variety is crowding out Daybreak wherever grown. 10c ea.; 60c per doz.; $4.00 per 100; $30.00 per 1,000.

Mrs. Geo. M. Bradt.—Clear white, heavily striped with scarlet; flowers of the largest size. Strong, vigorous grower. The most profitable variegated Carnation. 5c ea.; 50c per doz.; $3.00 per 100; $25.00 per 1,000.

Mrs. Jas. Dean.—Very large; clear, silvery pink; extra long, stiff stem; strong grower. With us this variety produces the largest and longest stemed flowers of any Carnation. 5c ea.; 35c per doz.; $2.00 per 100; $15.00 per 1,000.

Mrs. F. Jooste.—A beautiful shade of true, rose pink. A very strong grower, giving an abundance of large flowers on good stems. The best pink with many growers. 5c ea.; 35c per doz.; $2.00 per 100; $15.00 per 1,000.

Mrs. Thos. W. Lawson.—New of 1900. The largest pink Carnation at the present day. Color, clear cerise. Extra, long, stiff stem and perfect calyx. A strong and vigorous grower. This variety has proved all that was claimed for it, being not only of large size, but also very free. Will be grown by many as a commercial variety. 10c ea.; $1.00 per doz.; $7.00 per 100; $60.00 per 1,000.

Olympia.—New of 1900. A very large flower of ideal form and fine finish. Color, glossy snow white, very delicately penciled scarlet. Long, stiff stem; an excellent traveler and keeper; free from disease. A very profuse bloomer, producing more flowers than Mrs. Bradt. 10c ea.; 75c per doz.; $5.00 per 100; $40.00 per 1,000.

The Marquis.—New of 1900. The finest pink Carnation sent out for several years, being of a soft, rich shade of true pink, with no trace of purple or magenta. Very double, high rounded flower; petals beautifully serrated. It has the strong, perfect calyx of Albertina, its parent. Large flowers on stems 2 to 3 ft. long. Very fragrant. Excellent keeping qualities. A continuous bloomer, making no grass. Of exceptional merit, 10c ea.; 75c per doz.; $5.00 per 100; $40.00 per 1,000.

White Cloud.—May be briefly described as a white "Daybreak," of which it is a seedling. Very large, well filled flowers on stiff stems, 2 to 2½ ft. in length. Very free bloomer; the best white with many growers. 5c ea.; 40c per doz.; $2.50 per 100; $20.00 per 1,000.

Peru.—New of 1900. A very large Carnation of the purest white. Flowers of fine form and substance, fragrant and having a perfect calyx, which never burts. It is a strong grower and blooms very freely without cropping. 10c ea.; 75c per doz.; $5.00 per 100.

Canna Novelties for 1901.

Crozy's of 1900.

Strong Established Plants Only. Not less than 6 at dozen and 25 at 100 rate. Ready February 15th. Price, 50c each; $5.00 per dozen, except where noted.

C. Drevet.—Extra large flowers, borne in great profusion. Very similar to Mrs. Kate Gray in color. Height, 2½ ft. Very strong grower, with large, green foliage.

Chas. Molin.—Very strong foot-stalks, 3 ft. high; stools very freely. Extra large flower; pear shaped petals; flesh color, with darker veins at the center and a narrow margin of light yellow. Very striking.

Countess de Breteuil.—Bright pink, darker than Rosemawr. Very strong grower; heavy foliage; height, 2½ ft. Good for pot culture. An extra fine variety in every way.

J. Aymard.—Strong grower; good spike, well filled with flowers of medium size. Bright cerise, approaching scarlet; 3½ feet high. Very distinct.

Mme. Alfred Blanc.—Extra heavy growth and foliage. Large trusses of medium to large flowers. Color, deep salmon, with yellow shadings and a narrow yellow margin; free. Height, 3 ft. Very good.

Mme. Louis Druz.—Very bright scarlet; broad, rounded petals, forming a round flower very similar to Sam Trelease. Fine foliage; height, 3 ft. Does not sunburn. Very free bloomer.

Souv. de Mme. Nardy.—(Crozy of '99.) A fine, healthy grower; 4½ ft. high. Very broad petals; color, yellow ground, with large spots of bright crimson on the style of Florence Vaughan, but an improvement in every way. 15c ea.; $1.50 per doz.; $10.00 per 100.

One each of the above collection for $2.75.

New American Varieties.

Admiral Schley.—(Conard & Jones.) A very bold and showy variety, having large, broad petals and well opened flowers. Color, rich orange scarlet, spotted and dashed with bright crimson. Petals, banded rich golden yellow. Height, 3 ft. Very striking. 45c ea.; $4.80 per doz.

Betsey Ross.—(C. & J.) Named after the maker of the first American flag, owing to its many good points. Medium to large flowers; in color, a beautiful soft pink, which stands the sun well. A compact grower; 2⅝ ft. high. A very free bloomer. The trusses are large, erect and nicely placed above the foliage. The finest among all pink Cannas. 75c ea.; $6.00 per doz.

Cherokee.—(C. & J.) Color, a rich shade of dark maroon. Broad petals, soft and fine as velvet. The flowers are similar in form to Black Prince. Large, erect trusses, borne well above the foliage. A vigorous grower and always in bloom. An excellent bedding Canna; about 3 ft. high. 30c ea.; $3.00 per doz.

Montana.—(C. & J.) Flowers, bright creamy yellow; bears wind, sun and rain well. Even and regular growth, making fine trusses. Excellent for bedding and borders. 30c ea.; $3.00 per doz.

Niagara.—(C. & J.) The markings are somewhat like Gloriosa, but the flower and truss is uniformly larger. Center of petals, exceedingly bright crimson, bordered with deep golden yellow. As the amount of yellow varies on different flowers, the contrast produces a most showy and striking effect. 40c ea.; $3.50 per doz.

Queen of Holland.—(C. & J.) The most beautiful deep orange colored American hybrid Canna ever seen. Makes handsome plants, 2½ to 3 ft. high; purple foliage. Immense, branching trusses of deep orange colored flowers. Very novel and beautiful. 75c ea.; $6.00 per doz.

Striped Beauty.—(C. & J.) A most odd and interesting variety. Color, pretty buff, yellow, or creamy white, finely striped all over with soft, rich crimson. Moderate sized flowers on long, slender spikes. Green foliage. 40c ea.; $4.00 per doz.

West Grove.—(C. & J.) The nearest to a storm proof Canna ever grown. Storms that will spoil the flowers of all the leading Cannas will leave West Grove almost unharmed. An exceedingly strong, vigorous grower. Large, erect trusses, nicely placed above the foliage. Large, well shaped flowers of remarkable substance. The color is a rich coral pink, slightly dappled with bright crimson and yellow shadings at the throat. Very free. 45c ea.; $4.80 per doz.

One each of the above collection for $3.50, or one each of the above and Crozy's Novelties for $6.00.

Two New Orchid Flowered Hybrids.

Pennsylvania.—(C. & J.) A true hybrid, Duke of Marlborough being the seed parent. The flowers are as large as the largest of the Orchid flowering class, and the color is a deep, rich scarlet. Very free bloomer, six to eight large spikes in bloom at a time on a single plant, not being an uncommon sight. It blooms twice as free as any of the Orchid flowering varieties. Like this class of Cannas, it is a tall grower. Very large and abundant foliage. A grand Canna, which will easily become a leader. $1.00 ea.; $10.00 per doz.

Mrs. Kate Gray.—Another grand hybrid between the Orchid flowering and Crozy types. Very strong growth; large, bronzy green foliage; height 6 ft. Immense bright orange-scarlet flowers, which do not burn in the hottest weather. A very early, free and continuous bloomer. The spikes very often branch five and six times, thereby giving flowers from six to eight weeks from a single growth. Should be in every garden. 25c ea.; $2.50 per doz.

One each of the Orchid Flowered Hybrids and Crozy's Novelties will be furnished for $3.50.

One each of the Orchid Flowered Hybrids and New American Collection for $4.25, or one each of the above three collections for $7.00.

CANNAS OF RECENT INTRODUCTION.

Established Plants Only.   Ready March 1st.   Price, 10c each; $1.00 per dozen, except where noted.

Crimson Bedder.—Compact growth; height, 3 ft. Large trusses of well opened florets; color, bright crimson. Very early and free bloomer.

Golden Bedder.—What is said of Crimson Bedder applies to this variety, except that it is more dwarf in habit, attaining a height of 2½ ft., also has smaller florets. Bright golden yellow, with a faint trace of red at base of petals. Very free and early.

Golden Standard.—Height, about 4 ft. A very profuse bloomer; long spikes; color, pure chrome yellow, excepting an occasional slight vermillion tint on the lower petal. Excellent substance; does not burn very easily.

J. T. Lovett.—Very large, leathery leaves; height, 5 ft. Very large and long florets, set in a loose, open, drooping cluster. Color, a rich crimson lake. Free, continuous bloomer. Fine for massing.

Leopard.—Extremely stocky grower; height, 4 ft. Large, compact trusses of bright canary-yellow flowers, broadly blotched and spotted with rich crimson. A very early and free bloomer. Exceedingly unique and distinct.

Maple Avenue.—Growth of medium height, producing numerous long, compact spikes of orange vermillion flowers, with scarlet and crimson tints toward the calyx. Valuable for grouping.

Mottled Queen.—Large vermillion blotches on a pale yellow ground, the markings being so profuse as to frequently become confluent. A good bedder.

Mrs. Eisele.—A very vigorous grower, attaining a height of 5 to 7 ft., with abundant large foliage. Extra large florets; color, light salmon pink, distinct from any other variety; large, full trusses. Its novel color renders it of untold value.

Olympia.—An exceptionally good bedding Canna. It is a very free bloomer, bears large trusses nicely placed above the foliage and the flowers stand the sun very well. Color, violet purple, striped with crimson, showing a blue tinge after the flowers have been out several days. Entirely distinct. 15c ea.; $1.50 per doz.

Sunset.—A very charming border variety, attaining only a height of 20 in. to 24 in. Profuse bloomer; not unlike Mme. Crozy in color, but lighter, with a broader yellow band.

Villa de Poitiers.—Height, 2¼ ft. Very heavy growth. Color, a very rich shade of deep golden yellow, sometimes lightly splashed with red. Flower on the style of Sam. Trelease.

One each of the above collection for $1.00.

General Collection.

Prices quoted are for Strong, Dormant Roots. After Apr. 1st, established plants only, furnished at an advance of 30c per doz.; $2.00 per 100, on prices quoted.

Not less than 6 at doz., and 25 at 100 rate.

Alphonse Bouvier.—Height, 5 ft.; 2 to 3 flower spikes on one stalk. Bright crimson flowers in large, full spikes. One of the best crimson bedders. 5c ea.; 50c per doz.; $3.50 per 100.

Allemania.—Orchid flowering. This variety produces the largest flowers yet obtained in the way of Cannas. Height, 4 ft. The outer petals are dark orange with a very broad, golden yellow border. The best of this type. 10c ea.; 85c per doz.; $6.00 per 100.

Annie Laurie.—A charming and lovely variety, bearing large spikes of flowers, rivaling the finest Gladiolus in color, which is exquisite silvery rose, with a distinct white throat. Very beautiful, 2¼ ft. high. 15c ea.; $1.30 per doz.

Augusta.—(Cuba.) Very large florets; intense scarlet, widely bordered with clear golden yellow. Height, 3 ft. Largest gilt edge variety to date, and entirely distinct in color and form from all others. 10c ea.; 85c per doz.; $6.00 per 100.

Beaute Poitevine.—Rich, bright crimson flowers, on erect spikes, 3¼ ft. high. One of the best bedding Cannas. Very free bloomer. 10c ea.; $4.00 per 100.

Black Prince.—A seedling from the famous Duke of Marlborough, but darker in color. Intense, dark, velvety crimson, almost black. Enormous florets in large, bold trusses. Strong grower; 4 ft. high. Does not fade or burn. The best dark crimson to date. 15c ea.; $1.30 per doz.; $10.00 per 100.

Burbank.—Orchid flowering. A beautiful clear yellow of the largest size, showing crimson spots at the base of petals. Medium height and free flowering. The flowers are mostly semi-double. 5c ea.; 50c per doz.; $3.00 per 100.

Buttercup.—Clear, bright Buttercup yellow. Large, well formed flowers, in fine, open trusses; always clean and bright. Height, 3 ft. Does not sunburn or fade. Without doubt the best yellow Canna. Potted plants only, 15c ea.; $1.50 per doz.

Chas. Henderson.—Dark, rich crimson. Large, handsome spikes. Height, 3½ ft. A standard sort and a favorite in its color. 5c ea.; 50c per doz.; $3.50 per 100.

Directeur Roelz.—Rosy carmine; large flower; very robust grower, stooling freely; free bloomer. 5c ea.; 50c per doz.; $3.00 per 100.

Egandale.—Bright crimson; 3 to 4 ft. high. Deep bronze foliage. Unsurpassed for bedding, owing to its rapid growth and numerous branching trusses. 10c ea.; 75c per doz.; $5.00 per 100.

Explorateur Crampbel.—Cardinal red, with bright crimson splashings. Large, well filled spikes. Considered one of the most valuable of its color. Height, 4 ft. 5c ea.; 50c per doz.; $3.50 per 100.

Florence Vaughan.—Rich, golden yellow, thickly spotted with red. One of the finest variegated varieties. Very free; 4 ft. high. 10c ea.; 60c per doz.; $4.00 per 100.

Giant Crimson.—Five to six feet high. Color, intense glowing crimson. Very vigorous growth. An excellent bedder. 10c ea.; $1.00 per doz.

Gloriosa.—Dwarf, seldom exceeding 2 ft. in height. Immense trusses of rich, scarlet crimson flowers, margined with a broad yellow band. Unexcelled for pot culture or borders. 10c ea.; 85c per doz.; $6.00 per 100.

Martha Washington.—Very large flowers, frequently having five broad petals. Large, well filled trusses. A vigorous grower; height, 3 ft. Color, pure bright rose. This is the best pink Canna we have ever grown. 15c ea.; $1.30 per doz.; $10.00 per 100.

Mdlle. Berat.—An excellent bedder. Fine, bright pink flowers in large, well filled heads; long, gracefully drooping petals; Very free flowering. Height, 4 ft. Distinct in form and color. 10c ea.; 60c per doz.; $4.00 per 100.

Paul Marquant.—Bright salmon scarlet, with rich velvety lustre. Very strong grower; 3 ft. high. A popular pink with many. 5c ea.; 50c per doz.; $3.00 per 100.

Pierson's Premier.—Rich crimson scarlet, mottled and edged with yellow. Large, bold flowers in handsome trusses. A fine bedding variety. 10c ea.; 85c per doz.; $6.00 per 100.

Pres. Cleveland.—One of the finest scarlet bedders introduced for several years. Bright orange scarlet, very showy and handsome. A compact, vigorous grower, throwing up numerous trusses of large flowers. Height, 3 ft. 10c ea.; 60c per doz.; $4.00 per 100.

Queen Charlotte.—Rich crimson, with a broad margin of yellow. Extra strong grower. Although old, it is still one of the best of of its color. 10c ea.; 60c per doz.; $4.00 per 100.

Queen Eleanor.—The finest yellow spotted Canna. An improvement on Florence Vaughan in every way. Height, 3 to 4 ft. 10c ea.; 75c per doz.; $5.00 per 100.

Robusta.—A decorative variety, which with good cultivation will grow fully 10 ft. high. Very large leaves, of a bright bronzy color. Unequaled for tropical effect. 5c ea.; 50c per doz.; $3.00 per 100.

Rosemawr.—Extra large flowers, having broad, rounded petals frequently 2 in. across. The color is bright, rosy pink mottled with dark rose, shaded yellow at the throat. Immense trusses. Height, 3 ft. A very showy and handsome Canna. Established plants only, 15c ea.; $1.50 per doz.

Sam. Trelease.—This is one of the best gilt edge Cannas. Large, flat flowers; rounded petals. Color, bright scarlet, with narrow band of yellow. Strong grower. Height, 3 ft. 15c ea.; $1.50 per doz.; $8.00 per 100.

Souv. d'Antoine Crozy.—A fine gilt edged variety. Large, full spikes. Rich crimson flowers, bordered with golden yellow. Height, 2½ to 3 ft. A very popular Canna. 10c ea.; 60c per doz.; $4.00 per 100.

Souv. de Mme. Crozy.—Bright scarlet, bordered with rich golden yellow. A very strong grower, throwing up numerous trusses of the largest size. One of the showiest of the gilt edged class. Height, 3 ft. 10c ea.; 85c per doz.; $6.00 per 100.

One each of General Collection for $2.25.

MIXED CANNAS.—Those desiring a bed of mixed Cannas will be more than pleased with our stock, as it contains a large variety of the different shades and colors. 25c per doz.; $1.50 per 100.

New Geraniums.

The Tom Thumbs among Geraniums.

Mars.—A very dwarf and exceedingly free bloomer, the plants being entirely covered with medium sized trusses of single blooms. All buds should be removed from the plants while small, or they will exhaust themselves with blooming. Brilliant salmon pink at center, shading to white at margin. 10c ea.; 60c per doz.; $4.00 per 100.

America.—A seedling of Mars, having the same dwarf habit and freedom of bloom, but much stronger in growth. Opening blush white, the flowers become deep, pure rose when fully open, making a very beautiful and attractive truss. An ideal pot and bedding Geranium. 15c each; $1.50 per doz.; $8.00 per 100.

Little Pink.—(Hall.) Double pink Mars. The first double variety of this class. Same dwarf habit and freedom

LITTLE PINK.

of bloom as Mars; does not exceed 4 in. to 6 in. in height. Color bright pink, with no trace of salmon. This variety cannot be too highly recommended as a pot and bedding variety. 50c ea.; $5.00 per doz.; $35.00 per 100.

Eben E. Rexford.—(Eichholz.) Single. Light pink, white eye.

Dr. E. A. Hering.—(Eichholz.) Single. Brilliant scarlet, overlaid with red.

These two varieties are the ideal Geraniums we have been working on for years and there is nothing finer offered of foreign or domestic origin. They possess the dwarfness of Mars and America, but have the constitution and foliage of the Bruant type. Sunproof, brilliant in coloring and astonishingly floriferous. 25c ea.; $2.50 per doz.

Geraniums of Recent Introduction.

Not less than 6 at dozen, and 5 at 100 rate.

Andrew Lang.—Single bedder. Scarlet, with large white blotch on the upper petals; center of flower suffused with a rich tint of carmine. Extra strong grower, producing numerous large, well-filled trusses. 10c ea.; $1.00 per doz.

Cæsar.—Double. Rich red solferino. Clean, dwarf habit and a free bloomer. Very attractive and effective. A splendid acquisition. 5c ea.; $4.00 per 100.

C. W. Ward.—Heavy, compact growth; large, oval flowers; color, rich bronzy salmon; single. An excellent bedder. 10c ea.; $8.00 per 100.

Delavigne.—Single bedder. Beautiful light scarlet, with darker shadings toward center. Strong, upright grower and free. 10c ea.; $8.00 per 100.

Dr. Despres.—Double. Bright violet, with vermillion markings on upper petals, and the other segments marked scarlet. Very distinct. Excellent for pot culture, producing enormous flowers in great profusion. 10c ea.; $6.00 per 100.

Emanuel Arene.—Very large double florets. Pure white, with broad bands of rosy scarlet, making a flower of rare beauty. Extremely vigorous grower, producing an abundance of trusses set well above the foliage. This variety should be in every collection. 15c ea.; $10.00 per 100.

Hubert Charron.—A beautiful semi-double Auriole. Clear white center with a broad band of reddish carmine around each petal. A very showy variety and one of the finest in its class. This variety has given general satisfaction as a bedder, being a good grower and exceedingly free. 10c ea.; $6.00 per 100.

Jean Viaud.—Semi-double Bruant. Very strong growth with large foliage. The flowers are borne in immense trusses, which completely cover the plant from the time it is planted until frost. Color, a beautiful shade of bright rose, which does not fade in the hottest weather. This magnificent variety will supercede all pinks now on the market, as it is just as free as S. A. Nutt, and makes much larger trusses. 15c ea.; $10.00 per 100.

John P. Cleary.—Brilliant scarlet, single bedder. One of the finest in its class. Dwarf habit. 10c ea.; $1.00 per doz.

Kleber.—Double. Dark violet, rich and striking. Compact, sturdy growth. Free flowering. Very distinct. 5c ea.; $4.00 per 100.

La Fayette.—Large trusses of deep violet-crimson flowers. Very double. Dwarf, compact grower. Profuse bloomer. 10c ea.; $6.00 per 100.

La Fraicheur.—Double Picotee. Pure snow white, with a narrow, distinct edge of rosy pink. Very striking and unique. Dwarf, compact grower. No Florist should miss this variety. 10c ea.; $1.00 per doz.

Mathieu de Dombasle.—Double. Center salmon rose, bordered cream. Large trusses. Strong grower. A beautiful variety. 5c ea.; 50c per doz.

M. Canovas.—Double. Immense trusses of brilliant, fiery-scarlet flowers with velvet-maroon shadings. Fine, dwarf, spreading habit; very free. One of the darkest Geraniums we know of. 10c ea.; $5.00 per 100.

Mme Charotte.—Semi-double Bruant. One of the grandest sorts in this class. Dwarf, spreading habit. Distinct, pure salmon, occasionally veined with white. Extra large trusses with individual florets two inches and over in diameter. We consider this a decided improvement on Beautte Poitevine, being better color and more prolific. 20c ea.; $2.00 per doz.

Mme. H. Tilmant.—Semi-double. White center, with broad margin of scarlet, similar to H. Charron. A very attractive variety. 10c ea.; 75c per doz.

Mme. Landry.—Semi-double Bruant. Deep apricot salmon, darker than Beautte Poitevine. Fine dwarf habit and an exceedingly profuse bloomer. This variety has far exceeded our expectations, proving to be all that is claimed for it. Does not burn and is not effected by drought. 10c ea.; $8.00 per 100.

Pierre Le Brun.—Single bedder. Deep rose, veined bright carmine. Strong, vigorous grower and a free, continuous bloomer. A grand novelty and should be in every collection. 10c ea.; $6.00 per 100.

Ryecroft Pride.—Double crimson, similar in color to Meteor rose. Very large florets on strong stems. Very fine color. 10c ea.; $6.00 per 100.

Richelieu.—A valuable addition to the double crimson section, being the strongest grower in this class. Extra large trusses and long stems. Color, deep crimson maroon with dark orange center. 10c ea.; $8.00 per 100.

General Collection.

5c each; $3.50 per 100, except where noted.   Not less than 5 at 100 rate.

Beaute Poitevine.—Rosy salmon. One of the finest semi-doubles, having no equal in its color. Very large florets. 5c ea.; $4.00 per 100.

Claire Fromont.—Large trusses of enormous, semi-double florets. Color, beautiful rose pink without salmon or magenta shadings.

Countess de Castiers.—Large, double florets; pure pink. Strong, robust grower, producing an abundance of trusses from Spring until Frost. Is not effected by dry weather. An excellent bedder. 5c ea.; $4.00 per 100.

Duchess de Maillen.—Double salmon pink, lighter than Wm. Phitzer, but a stronger grower.

Duc de Montemart.—Velvety carmine. Dwarf and exceedingly free flowering. Double: very large florets. This is one of the best bedders we have. 5c ea.; $4.00 per 100.

H. Dauthenay.—Bruant type. Dwarf and robust grower. Single; orange red with white eye. Exceedingly free. 5c ea.; $4.00 per 100.

J. Ricaud.—A very free flowering variety, with long stems and enormous trusses of intense purplish crimson flowers. Extra strong grower.

La Favorite.—Double white. A general favorite as a bedding and market variety. 5c ea.; $3.00 per 100.

L'Aube.—Extra large trusses of pure snow white flowers. A very profuse bloomer. Single. 5c ea.; $4.00 per 100.

Marguerite Pinon.—Clear rose pink, with violet and dark rose shadings. Double. Very beautiful and distinct. One of the best.

Marvel.—Double crimson bedder. A healthy and vigorous grower. Grown by many in place of S. A. Nutt. 5c ea.; $3.00 per 100.

M. Alphonse Ricard.—Bruant type. Clear orange red. If not already in your collection, do not fail to secure this superb variety. Free flowering. Dwarf, sturdy habit, and as a bedder is unsurpassed. 5c ea.; $4.00 per 100.

Marguerite de Layre.—The finest single white. A favorite with many. 5c ea.; $4.00 per 100.

Mme. Debouche.—A grand variety. Large, double florets; rose, shading to light pink. Dwarf, robust habit. An excellent bedder. 5c ea.; $4.00 per 100.

Mme. Jaulin.—Bruant type. Delicate pink, bordered with pure white. Entirely distinct in color. A fine bedder. Very popular. 5c ea.; $4.00 per 100.

Mme. Buchner.—Double white. More vigorous constitution than La Favorite and just as free flowering. Exceedingly strong, robust growth.

Mme. Bruant.—White, veined with carmine lake. Very distinct and striking. Single. Exceedingly free flowering. 5c ea.; $3.00 per 100.

Mrs. E. G. Hill.—Single. Soft light salmon, changing to rosy salmon. Perfect habits. 10c ea.; $5.00 per 100.

Ruy Blas.—Double bedder. Salmon center, peach rose border. Very desirable for pot culture. One of the finest of its color.

Sam. Sloan.—Light crimson, single bedder. Large trusses, borne in profusion. Although old, it is still one of the best.

S. A. Nutt.—The best double crimson to date. 5c ea.; $3.00 per 100.

Theo. Theulier.—Single bedder. Brilliant scarlet. Fine habit.

Van Beneden.—Fine, large flowers; lower petals rich violet crimson; upper petals bright orange scarlet. Single. An excellent bedder.

Wm. Phitzer.—Bright apricot, shading to salmon at the edges of the petals; double. Very free flowering. One of the best of its color.

New Pelargoniums.

Price, 20c each; $2.00 per dozen, except where noted.

Bridegroom.—A very pleasing shade of rosy blush, tinted maroon. Beautifully crimped flowers. Dwarf and very free. 30c ea.; $3.00 per doz.

Crimson King.—For freedom of bloom, depth of color and good habit, we do not hesitate to predict that it will become one of the most popular varieties for market purposes. As its name implies, it is of a most intense crimson color. 30c ea.; $3.00 per doz.

Evening Star.—Deep crimson, spotted and blotched. Pure white throat. Exceedingly free flowering.

Joseph Leigh.—Clear rosy pink, with large, dark maroon blotch on upper petals. Very dwarf habit and free flowering.

Linda.—A remarkably free blooming Pelargonium, producing large trusses of elegantly fringed flowers. Color, beautiful orange pink, upper petals feathered with maroon. A grand variety.

Prince George.—Enormous trusses of finely fringed white flowers, faintly suffused with blush, all the petals spotted with maroon. A very attractive and distinct flower.

Purity.—A very early bloomer. Color, pure white, with pink spots on upper petals. Very large trusses; robust constitution. A good Winter bloomer.

General Collection.

10c each; $8.00 per 100. Not less than 5 plants at 100 rate.

Capt. Raikes.—Flowers very large and full. Color, dark fiery crimson; crisp petals of great substance. The best of its color.

Innocente.—A grand flower of good substance, one-half again as large as any other white Pelargonium. Beautifully frimbriated; pure white. Fine for design work. Very dwarf.

Mme. Thibaut.—The Queen of Pelargoniums. Light rose blotches on white ground; double. One of the best for Florists' use.

Mme. Vibert.—Ground color rose, almost covered with brilliant black maroon blotches; light center and edges. Very beautiful.

Mrs. Robt. Sandiford.—The finest double white. Snow white flowers, with beautifully ruffled edges.

Robt. Green.—Extra strong, robust growth. Medium sized flowers. Color, clear rose pink, lower petals having a dark maroon blotch.

Sandiford's Best.—A beautiful shade of pink, surrounded with a broad band of white; large white throat. Produces an abundance of large, well-filled trusses. A very distinct and attractive variety.

Sandiford's Surprise.—Large, black blotches on upper petals; edge, fiery red, surrounded with a broad band of white. Lower petals white, spotted bright red. One of the most distinct in cultivation.

Sandiford's Wonder.—Splendid semi-double, pure white flowers, some showing a rich maroon spot in upper petals; heavily fringed. A genuine Florists' Pelargonium. The plants are covered with blooms throughout the entire season.

Victor.—Color, bright cherry pink; white at base of petals, upper petals blotched deep crimson maroon. One of the best, and a favorite with many.

Two New Roses.

QUEEN OF EDGELY.

Queen of Edgely.—(Floral Exchange.) The long looked for "pink" American Beauty, being a sport from that popular variety. It is an exact counterpart of American Beauty in every particular, except that of color. It has the same vigorous growth and beautiful foliage of the parent plant. Its fragrance is delicious and closely resembles that of the out-door June Roses. In color, it is a bright pink, approaching Mme. Caroline Testout and Bridesmaid. An excellent point is, that as the Rose grows older, it fades to a lovely shade of light pink. The flowers are large and deep, cup shaped and full, averaging 5 in. when fully developed (some reaching 7 in. in diameter). They are borne on stems often 6 ft. long, with foliage to the flower. Its keeping qualities are excellent, the flowers keeping for a week or longer after being cut. Winner of numerous medals and certificates of merit. No person should fail to secure a stock of this beautiful Rose. Disseminated during April. Strong plants from 2½ in. pots, $1.00 ea.; $9.00 per doz.; $25.00 for 50; $40.00 per 100. Larger plants quoted on application.

4

Sunrise.—(Hill Co.) The most gorgeous Tea Rose yet introduced. In close bud form, it shows the high, brilliant colors, seen only in the "Austrian Copper," scarlet and yellow. Both the red and yellow deepen as the flower opens. The open rose is large, perfectly double and of grand form. Thick, glossy foliage. The new growths are the darkest and most beautiful found among Roses. Its freedom of growth and bloom, and the exquisite color, will give it a high place among forcing Roses. Has taken first honors wherever shown, both here and abroad. Strong plants from 2¼ in. pots, 20c ea.; $15.00 per 100.

NEPHROLEPIS WITTBOLDII.

A Valuable New Sword Fern.

Nephrolepis Wittboldii.—(Wittbold.) The most valuable addition to the Nephrolepis family since the introduction of Neph. Bostoniensis. Very robust and graceful grower, and is one of the most prolific Ferns in existence, equaling, if not excelling the Bostoniensis in beauty. Long, graceful fronds, with broad, undulated pinnates. A most desirable Fern for Florists' use. Strong, thrifty plants, ready for 3 and 4 in. pots, $1.00 ea.; $10.00 per doz.; $75.00 per 100.

Two of the Most Pop= ular Begonias.

Ready for Delivery in June.

Gloire de Lorraine.—This is one of the most striking plants that has been introduced for many years. Very compact, dwarf habit, making handsome specimens 14 in. in height and breadth. The plant is completely covered with its brilliant, clear pink flowers to such an extent that the foliage is usually hidden. It has been successfully grown by many for Christmas sales, and brought very high prices. It is undoubtedly one of the most useful Christmas plants now in existence, owing to its extreme floriferousness. Its chief requirements are a soil composed of well rotted sods and leaf mold, and a warm, moderately dry atmosphere, with an abundance of ventilation. Produces the most useful and durable plants in an atmosphere at from 60 to 70 degrees, but the foliage must be kept dry. As it requires the temperature of a living room, it can be successfully grown as a house plant. 20c ea.; $15.00 per 100.

Light Pink Lorraine.—(Lonsdale's Variety.) A beautiful light pink sport from the above variety. A counterpart, except in color. Entirely distinct and vastly superior to Nana Compacta. 30c ea.; $25.00 per 100.

PINK GLOIRE DE LORRAINE.

DATE OF DELIVERY, EARLY IN JUNE. The most successful growers of these Begonias agree that strong, **STURDY PLANTS CANNOT BE DELIVERED BEFORE JUNE 1st.** This stock will produce strong plants, in 5 and 6 in., or even larger pots, for Christmas trade. Let us book your order for delivery at the proper time.

Violets.

Price, 5c each; $3.00 per 100.   Rooted Runners Quoted on Application.

Double.

Imperial.—Large, and very double flowers. In color, the darkest blue grown. Exceedingly healthy, vigorous growth, making an abundance of flowers. An improvement on Marie Louise.

Lady Hume Campbell.—Lighter in color than Marie Louise; free grower and productive. A grand variety for house culture. Does best when grown a few degrees warmer than other Violets.

Marie Louise.—A favorite with many and the most extensively grown double Violet. Large, double, deep blue flowers.

Swanley White.—Flowers double and pure white; good constitution and free flowering. The best double white. Very healthy grower.

Single.

California.—Vigorous plant, absolutely free from disease, producing an abundance of long stemmed flowers. Hardy. Very dark blue.

Princess of Wales.—The most popular among single Violets. The petals are wider than those of other varieties, resembling those seen in Pansies; the flowers being nearly as large as a silver dollar. Color, true violet blue; very productive. One of the best for Winter forcing.

White Czar.—Strong grower; very free bloomer. The best single white.

Miscellaneous.

Asparagus Plumosus Nanus.—(Lace Fern.) A very graceful climber, succeeding under almost any condition. Unsurpassed for decorating, and is rapidly taking the place of Smilax, as it is a better keeper and has finer foliage. One of the most useful Florists' plants. 10c ea.; $5.00 per 100.

Asparagus Sprengerii.—(Emerald Feather.) One of the most desirable varieties among this class of plants, being especially useful for pot plants and hanging baskets. Excellent for house culture, as the dry air does not affect it. No Florist should be without it. 10c ea.; $5.00 per 100.

Asparagus Tenuissimus.—Fine foliage, similar to Plumosus. Useful as a window plant, being of easy culture. 10c ea.; $4.00 per 100.

Begonia Rex.—One of the most beautiful foliage plants for house and conservatory. Our collection includes the best standard varieties. 10c ea.; $5.00 per 100.

Begonia Incarnata.—This is one of the best varieties among Begonias, being of the easiest culture and very free flowering. Extra good for bush form; fine foliage. Light pink flowers, which completely hide the foliage when the plant is in full bloom. As it is at its best the latter part of December, its value as a Christmas plant may be readily seen. 5c ea.; $4.00 per 100.

Bougainvillea Glabra Sanderiana.—Rosy crimson flowers produced in abundance. Equally valuable, either as a bush plant or climber. To grow shapely bush plants they should be pruned occasionally. A very useful plant. Strong, bushy plants from 3¼ in. pots. 10c ea.: $8.00 per 100.

Carax Japonica Variegata.—A variegated grass very desirable for borders, rockeries and basket work. It also makes a very pretty plant for the table or conservatory. It is quite hardy and not easily affected by drought; 10 in. high. One of the most useful decorative plants we have. 5c ea.; $4.00 per 100.

Cyclamen.—Our stock is grown from the best selected European strain of seed. being of the large flowering type. Separate colors. We will have fine plants for Easter trade and the young stock for next Winter's blooms will be ready in August. 10c ea.; $5.00 a 100.

Cyperus Alternifolius.—(Umbrella Plant.) A decorative plant of easy culture. 5c ea.; $3.00 per 100.

Ferns.—NEPHROLEPIS CORDATA COMPACTA.—A very fine Fern for house culture, being a free grower. Growth very compact, dwarf, and of a beautiful deep green. 5c ea.; $4.00 per 100.

NEPH. CORDIFOLIA.—Dwarf habit; strong, vigorous grower. One of the best. 5c ea.; $4.00 per 100.

NEPH. EXELTATA.—A very graceful, strong growing variety of rugged constitution, thriving under all conditions. Very long fronds. 10c ea.; $6.00 per 100.

NEPH. EX. BOSTONIENSIS.—(Boston Fern.) One of the best and most popular Ferns in existence; long, arching fronds, 2 to 3 ft. in length. Growth similar to that of Exeltata. Of very easy culture. 5c ea.; $4.00 per 100.

NEPH. WITTBOLDII.—(For description and price see page 26.)

Feverfew.—(Matricaria.) An indispensable plant to the Florists, being very useful for cutting and floral work. 5c ea.; $2.50 per 100.

Geraniums.—ROSE SCENTED.—5c ea.; $3.00 per 100.

MME. SALLEROI.—Small leaves, variegated green and white. A very popular border plant and quite extensively used for ornamental bedding. 5c ea.; $2.50 per 100.

Hydrangea.—OTASKA.—A beautiful Japanese variety used extensively for Easter decorations. Large heads of bright pink flowers. 5c ea.; $3.00 per 100.

THOS. HOGG.—Medium sized trusses of pure white flowers. Not as tall as Otaska, but much freer bloomer. 5c ea.; $3.00 per 100.

Ipomea.—(Moonflower.) A beautiful Summer climber 15 to 20 ft. high; makes excellent shade for verandas, also used for covering lattice work. Large, trumpet-shaped snow white flowers. 5c ea.; $4.00 per 100.

Isolepis Gracilis.—A grass-like plant very useful for ferneries and hanging baskets. Long, reed-like drooping blades, center erect. 5c ea.; $4.00 per 100.

Lemon Verbena.—The leaves are delightfully fragrant and refreshing. 5c ea.; $3.00 per 100.

Primula.—CHINESE.—Single, in separate colors. 10c ea.; $5.00 a 100. Ready Aug. 1.

OBCONICA.—(Frimbriatum & Hybridum.) 10c ea.; $5.00 per 100.

FORBESII.—(Baby Primrose.) 5c ea.; $4.00 per 100.

[The above Primulas are from the best selected European strains. After several years of careful selection, we are now in position to offer our customers a superior strain, which is giving the best of satisfaction wherever grown.]

Smilax.—Strong plants from 2¼ in. pots. 5c ea.; $2.50 per 100.

Sweet Alyssum.—Double; far superior to the single variety. 5c ea.; $2.50 per 100.

Vinca Major Variegata.—Glossy, green leaves, broadly margined and blotched creamy white. One of the very best trailing plants for vases and other filling where vines may be used. 5c ea.; $3.00 per 100.

Strong, dormant field grown clumps, extra fine for Spring work, from 3½ in. pots, 10c ea.; $8.00 per 100.

HARDY PERENNIALS.

Anemones.—(Windflower.) JAPONICA ALBA.—Large, single, pure white flowers. The best of its color. 10c ea.; $5.00 per 100.

QUEEN CHARLOTTE.—This is the greatest acquisition to this class of plants in many years. A beautiful shade of light rose pink. The plant is more robust than any of the old varieties and commences to bloom much earlier. Semi-double flowers, frequently 4 in. across. Should be in every collection. 10c ea.; $5.00 per 100.

Hardy Pinks.—In variety. 5c ea.; $3.00 per 100.

Helianthus.—(Hardy Sunflower.) MULTIFLORUS MAXIMUS.—A very large single variety, growing from 5 to 6 ft. high. Single, golden-yellow flowers often 6 to 8 in. across. One of the best. 10c ea.; $5.00 per 100.

Phalaris Variegata.—(Ribbon Grass.) A very useful variegated grass for bordering large beds. 5c ea.; $3.00 per 100.

Physostegia.—VIRGINICA ALBA.—One of the most beautiful of the midsummer flowering perennials, forming large bushes 3 to 4 ft. high. Long spikes of tubular flowers; color, pure white. 10c ea.; $5.00 per 100.

Rudbeckia.—GOLDEN GLOW.—A very showy hardy perennial growing 6 to 7 ft. high and producing an abundance of double, bright yellow flowers, which resemble those of the Dahlia in size and general appearance. 5c ea.; $3.00 per 100.

NEWMANII.—Dark orange-yellow flowers, with deep purple cone. Long, stiff stem, making it valuable for cutting. 10c ea.; $5.00 per 100.

PURPUREA.—One of the most interesting plants among hardy perennials. It is of easy culture, forming large, bushy plants, which produce a constant succession of large, reddish-purple flowers about 4 in. across. Large, brown, cone-shaped center, thickly set with golden tips. 10c ea.; $6.00 per 100.

Tritoma.—(Torch Lily.) PFITZERII.—An improvement on Uvaria Grandiflora. The flower spikes are more freely produced than in the older variety, being frequently 4 ft. high, with heads of bloom 12 in. long. Rich orange-scarlet, shading to salmon-rose on the edge. 10c ea.; $6.00 per 100.

UVARIA GRANDIFLORA.—Orange-red flowers. 5c ea.; $4.00 per 100.

CHOICE CANNA SEED.

This seed was saved from our large collection of Cannas, including Novelties, and embraces all the different shades and colors now found in this popular plant. Per packet, 5c; per ounce, 15c.

❧ How to Grow Chrysanthemums. ❧

Eighty-two pages, well illustrated. A practical compilation of matter contributed by many of the leading experts of the day. It contains cultural instructions for each month in the year, also chapters on Training, Diseases, Seed Saving, Etc., Etc.

Every grower of Chrysanthemums should procure this valuable work, as it treats on all subjects relative to the successful culture of The Queen of Autumn. Prepaid, by mail, only 25c. **Net.**

x   x   x

Chrysanthemum Culture for America.

History of the Chrysanthemum; Classification and Care. By James Morton.

An excellent and thorough book, especially adapted to the Culture of Chrysanthemums in America. Illustrated, 120 pages. Prepaid, by mail, 60c. **Net.**

x   x   x

❧ Wire Plant Supports. ❧

Our **Double Arch Carnation Support** is giving satisfaction wherever used. After trying very near every other method in use, we have come to the conclusion that this support is the best and cheapest Write for particulars and prices.

We can also supply **Rose** and **Chrysanthemum Stakes,** straightened and cut to any length.

We are in position to give you best value, as we procure our stock from one of the largest wire goods manufacturers in the country.

Prices will be regulated according to market value of wire at the time of quotation.

x   x   x

☞ERRATA.—Price of Carnation **Genevieve Lord,** on **Page 18,** should read: 10c each; 75c per dozen; $5.00 per 100; $40.00 per 1,000.

ADRIAN TIMES PRINT.

When possible, please remit by

Express Money Orders

Issued at Agencies of all Express Companies, payable in the United States, at following rates :

Not Over	- $2.50 .... 3 cts.	Over $30.00 to $40.00 ......15 cts.	
Over $ 2.50 to 5.00 .... 5 cts.	" 40.00 to 50.00 ......18 cts.	
" 5.00 to 10.00 .... 8 cts.	" 50.00 to 60.00 .....20 cts.	
" 10.00 to 20.00 ....10 cts.	" 60.00 to 75.00 .....25 cts.	
" 20.00 to 30.00 ....12 cts.	" 75.00 to 100.00 ......30 cts.	

Two cents in addition to the above rates will be collected for cost of Revenue Stamp required by the War Tax.

MEMORANDUM
FOR USE WHEN YOU REMIT || Fill out blank spaces below and send or take this memorandum to nearest Express Agency, with amount of order and charges.

Amount of Order

Payable to {

Nathan Smith & Son,

Adrian, Mich.

$..................................

Name of Sender..

THIS IS THE CHEAPEST, SAFEST AND MOST CONVENIENT WAY TO SEND MONEY.

CPSIA information can be obtained
at www.ICGtesting.com
Printed in the USA
BVHW041731051118
532208BV00024B/4849/P